How to
Talk
Dinosaur
with Your
Child

How to Talk Dinosaur with Your Child

Q. L. PEARCE

Lowell House
Los Angeles

Contemporary Books
Chicago

Library of Congress Cataloging-in-Publication Data

Pearce, Q. L. (Querida Lee)
    How to talk dinosaur with your child / text by Q.L. Pearce.
      p.   cm.
    Includes bibliographical references and indcx.
    ISBN 0-929923-48-0
    1. Dinosaurs—Popular works.   2. Dinosaurs—Study and teaching.
I. Title.
QE862.D5P42   1991
567.9'1—dc20   91-26322
                                                      CIP

Requests for such permissions should be addressed to:
Lowell House
2029 Century Park East, Suite 3290
Los Angeles, CA 90067

Publisher: Jack Artenstein
Vice-President/Editor-in-Chief: Janice Gallagher
Director of Marketing: Elizabeth Duell Wood
Design: Tanya Maiboroda

Manufactured in the United States of America
10 9 8 7 6 5 4 3 2 1

To William J. Pearce, Ph.D.,
for his limitless encouragement and support.

Acknowledgments

I would like to express my thanks to those who graciously shared their knowledge and insights, and contributed to this book through interviews or correspondence: Robert T. Bakker, Adjunct Curator of Paleontology at the University of Colorado Museum; Edwin H. Colbert, Honorary Curator, Museum of Northern Arizona; Alan Cvancara, Professor of Geology, University of North Dakota; Steven Czerkas and Sylvia Czerkas, S & S Czerkas Studios; Peter Dodson, Associate Professor of Anatomy, School of Veterinary Medicine, University of Pennsylvania; John Horner, Curator of Paleontology, Museum of the Rockies, Montana State University; Grant Meyer, former curator of the Raymond M. Alf Museum of Claremont, California; Walter E. Reed, Professor of Geology, University of California at Los Angeles; Raymond T. Rye II, Museum Specialist, Department of Paleobiology, National Museum of Natural History; and Dave Swingle, Director of Education, Museum of the Rockies, Montana State University. I would also like to express my appreciation to Peggy Kayser, former Coordinator for Children's Programs at the Ralph M. Parsons Discovery Center, Natural History Museum of Los Angeles County, and current Museum Administrator at Hebrew Union College, Skirball Museum of Los Angeles, for her careful reading of this manuscript and for her valuable comments, and to L. Spencer Humphrey and Janice Gallagher for their patience and fine editorial assistance.

Contents

PART TWO: EXPLORING THE NEW AGE
OF DINOSAURS WITH YOUR CHILD

WHY DINOSAURS?
A Note to Parents

Long ago, across a great gulf of time more than 650,000 centuries wide, the last of the dinosaurs toppled to the ground releasing its final breath in a soft sigh. For the moment, the curtain had fallen on one of the most remarkable periods in Earth's history . . . the age of dinosaurs. The ill-fated beasts and others like them rested in the earth, virtually undisturbed for countless millennia, until, less than two centuries ago, a fragment—a tooth—came to light, sending the curtain up on a new age of dinosaurs. Granted, this second act lacks the active participation of its stars, but the players and the audience are undaunted. Although no one has ever seen or heard a living dinosaur, no animal has so gripped the human imagination. Children in particular are fascinated by dinosaurs. Unlike cartoon character fads, the love affair with these extraordinary creatures will continue to last as kids learn more and more about their favorites.

In his book *The Riddle of the Dinosaur,* John Noble Wilford wrote that "More than most other people, paleontologists, particularly those that hunt dinosaur bones, trace their careers back to their childhood." As a child, I, too, was captivated by the lure of the dinosaurs. I can't be certain whether it was their size and strength, or the mystery that surrounded them, but that interest (perhaps even affection) for these incredible animals led to a general curiosity about science. I wondered how scientists were able to learn about animals that existed millions of years before humans walked the earth, how they knew where to look for fossils, and for that matter, what fossils were? In searching for the answers, I soon discovered a remarkable thing. Science is fun! Now, as the author of numerous children's books on the subject of science, I have discovered something else—it is a wonderful adventure to share. Therein lies my main goal in writing this book—to provide parents with a clear, simple guide that will enable them to share their youngster's enthusiasm for dinosaurs, and also encourage an interest in the basic science that has brought the dinosaur age to life.

Part One is an overview of the dinosaur world, the animals that populated it, and the tireless scientists who have risked everything from attacks by hostile natives, assaults by hungry insects, sunburn, and even frostbite, to study it. A working knowledge in this area will help you answer your child's questions, as well as clear up any misconceptions. For example, cartoons, movies, and comic books sometimes mix dinosaurs of different eras, giving a youngster the incorrect impression that the animals coexisted. In fact, there is a greater expanse of time between Triassic dinosaurs, such as *Saltopus*, and Cretaceous animals, such as *Tyrannosaurus rex*, than there is between *Tyrannosaurus* and humans. Cartoons and films to the contrary, humans and dinosaurs did *not* coexist.

Indeed, the modern view of the dinosaur may be quite unlike what you learned as a child. When the existence of dinosaurs first came to light in the early to mid-1800's, they were generally depicted as vigorous, active animals. This view eventually fell into disfavor, and by the 1930's the public perception of the creatures was one of slow, rambling, dim-witted leviathans that did little more than eat, fight, and loll about in the mud. However, research over the past two decades paints a far different picture, one of active, intelligent animals of every size and shape. Evidence from fossils suggests that many dinosaurs built nests and cared for their young. Some had complex social structures, and certain varieties may have migrated in great thundering herds. In the past 20 years alone, almost a hundred new dinosaurs have been discovered in Mongolia, China, Brazil, Argentina, the United States, Canada, and other areas. The more we learn about these marvelous reptiles, the more we realize what truly intriguing creatures they were. It's easy to see why the current perception of the dinosaur is greeted by youngsters with such excitement and with an understanding of your child's object of enthusiasm, you will be better able to open up the entire world of science in a stimulating and appealing manner.

Determination, commitment, patience, perseverance—traits that make a good paleontologist—apply equally to all scientific endeavors. Curiosity and imagination are invaluable tools not only in the sciences but in any undertaking. Paleontology may not become a lifelong pursuit for your youngster just because he or she can easily recite multisyllabic dinosaur names or has begun to systematically excavate the backyard. However, even a fleeting fascination with these ancient animals and their world can be directed to nurture a child's natural curiosity. Throughout this book you will find sidebars featuring questions your child might ask, suggestions for questions that you could ask your youngster, and activities designed to help you to explain certain concepts to your child and to encourage further exploration.

Part Two outlines activities and offers recommendations for getting "into the field" yourself. Your child's interest in dinosaurs provides plenty of opportunities for simple, nondemanding situations through which you can learn together. For example, when reading newspapers or magazines, keep an eye open for articles about new discoveries and prepare a dinosaur "current events" file. Fossil hunting as an activity during a beach, river, or lakeside picnic, or during a hike in the mountains, can be fun for the whole family. Planning and executing a field trip helps a child to develop organizational skills, promotes attention to detail, and prompts a youngster to anticipate and prepare for possibilities. Besides putting a child in touch with the natural world, the rigors of a search for specimens encourages critical observation. When you visit a museum, take along a drawing pad and pencils. View the fossil exhibits together, then ask your child to draw a picture of what the animals looked like when they were alive. Speculating about a dinosaur's outward appearance and daily life is a worthwhile exercise. In reaching for answers, children stretch their imaginations.

Part Two also offers suggestions for throwing a dinosaur-themed birthday party—from instructions for festive decorations to recipes for delectable treats. To add to the amusement, I've provided a section on translating "dinosaurese," and a "quick reference" list of short, simple answers to the top 20 questions most often asked about dinosaurs.

This book is meant as a tool to help you open your child's mind to the thrills of the natural world around us. The most important thing to remember is to have fun. Whether your youngster's infatuation with dinosaurs is lasting or not, the love of learning for its own sake, once fired, is likely to be unquenchable.

How to
Talk
Dinosaur
with Your
Child

PART ONE

The World of Dinosaurs

1

What Is a Dinosaur?

On a visit to the Natural History Museum of Los Angeles County, I stopped to marvel at the exhibit of one of the most splendid *Tyrannosaurus rex* skulls on display in the world. A man nearby gripped his young son's hand and remarked, "That must have been some big lizard." Well, yes . . . and no. *Tyrannosaurus rex* was among the largest of the meat-eating dinosaurs, but it was not a lizard. I've also heard adults refer to any huge, ancient reptile as a "dinosaur." That, too, is off the mark. The dinosaurs were one of several large reptile groups that roamed the earth generally between 225 and 65 million years ago (MYA). Although they had certain traits in common with other reptiles, dinosaurs were unique unto themselves.

In order to study living things, scientists have organized all plants, animals, and those organisms somewhere inbetween, into groups according to shared characteristics. The largest of these divisions is the Kingdom, followed by the progressively smaller divisions of Phylum, Class, Order, Family, Genus, and Species. (To remember this, I use a sentence I learned in high school, "King Philip Came Over For Good Shoes." I believe the original sentence was actually a little racier, but this will work just as well.) The further down the line you go, the more characteristics group members have in common. For example, the profile of the family dog would look like this:

Kingdom	Animal
Phylum	Chordata
Class	Mammalia
Order	Carnivora
Family	Canidae
Genus	*Canis*
Species	*familiaris*

The phylum Chordata includes the dog, bird, mouse, human, lizard, dinosaur, and any other creature with a backbone or notochord (a long, flexible rod of cells). Dinosaurs part company with Rover at the class level. Although some scientists feel that dinosaurs deserve to be in a separate class (Archosauria) with certain other ancient reptiles and birds, they are presently considered Reptilia. Archosauria is often used as a subclass that includes dinosaurs, crocodiles, pterosaurs, and thecodonts (THEE-koh-donts).

> **With your child:** You can help your child to understand how this grouping system works by gathering a number of small objects, such as soap, scissors, a pen, a can of vegetables, a bag of chips, a fork, a sock, and so on, and placing them in a large box. Include pictures or clippings of a wide variety of plants and animals to represent living things.
>
> Have your youngster categorize the objects. He or she could start with two major groups: living things (represented by pictures or clippings) and nonliving things. Now move on to the nonliving group and break it into smaller groups: food, tools, and clothing, for example. Single out tools and find ways to group them—tools that cut, tools for writing, tools to eat with. There are no right or wrong answers here as long as the criteria are logical and consistent. As the groups get smaller it may be a little more difficult to categorize, and details become more important. When the project is completed, your child will be able to fit any object in the house into its proper category and will have a basic understanding of the value of taxonomy.

The first reptiles developed roughly around 300 MYA during the Late Pennsylvanian Period. They were more advanced than the only other land vertebrates of that time, the amphibians. When vertebrate animals left the sea and struggled out onto dry land, many new problems arose. Although most amphibians had successfully broken away from a full-time aquatic environment, they were still fettered to their watery world. They needed to keep their skin moist, and they had to lay their fragile eggs in water or damp places to prevent the shell-less orbs from drying out. So, although there was vertebrate life on earth when the reptiles made their entrance, it was generally limited to the sea and swamps and their margins.

Your child may ask: Why did animals leave the sea?

There are two possibilities, and both are based on the idea that the sea was a pretty crowded place. Perhaps the danger posed by large numbers of sea-going predators forced the first pioneering fish (possibly lobe-finned fish) to struggle into the safer shallows and eventually onto dry land. Another view is that these animals were searching for food, and the insects that lived along the shoreline slowly tempted them ashore.

For reptiles, the key to freedom took a simple but extraordinary form—the amniotic egg. This egg was as important to the reptilian conquest of the earth as the invention of the wheel was to humans. With its fully contained life-support system and porous but protective shell, a reptilian egg could be deposited in a wide variety of environments from wetlands to deserts. Of course, reptiles had already adapted to the demands of life on land by developing such characteristics as scaly skin with a horny outer layer to prevent water loss, and a new, more efficient mode of breathing. Amphibians have a sort of throat pump that forces air into the lungs. The reptiles developed a new method in which the rib cage was expanded and contracted to suck in air and push it out of the lungs. Still life on dry land for these first scaly residents had its drawbacks. Early reptiles were probably not very fast-moving. Their limbs extended laterally from the body, then turned down at the elbow or knee. This arrangement gave the creatures a sprawling posture, and some virtually crawled on their bellies. In addition, they were ectothermic, or cold-blooded. That means that their body temperature was not controlled internally, as in mammals and birds, but rather externally. Even in comparatively warm, equable conditions of the Pennsylvanian and Permian periods, reptilian body temperatures were subject to the changes in their immediate environment. Thus, the reptiles alternately basked or sought shade to maintain an optimum body temperature.

Near the close of the Paleozoic Era, during the Late Permian Period, a new group of reptiles emerged—the thecodonts. Thecodont means "socket-toothed," and indeed, thecodont teeth grew from small sockets in the jaw rather than from the surface of the jawbone as in earlier reptiles. One suborder in particular, the Ornithosuchia (or-nith-oh-SOOK-ee-uh), or "bird crocodiles," seemed quite capable of walking on their hind legs (which were decidedly longer than their forelegs) and could adopt a semierect rather than a sprawling posture. Ornithosuchians probably spent most of their time on all fours, but when necessary they could rise up on two legs and outrun both predators and competitors for food. *Lagosuchus* (lah-goh-SOOK-us), or "rabbit crocodile," was a particularly small, slender Ornithosuchian not much more than a foot long. This little animal, or one of its very close relatives, was probably the ancestor of the dinosaurs.

> **With your child:** Let your youngster decide which stance is more efficient. First, have your child bend over (as if to touch his or her toes) and put his or her hands on the floor. Then ask the child to lower his or her body, bending the elbows and knees outward. Tell your youngster to walk several steps forward and stop. Have your child straighten up so he or she is standing on two legs with the knees only slightly bent, then take a few steps forward again. Is this way easier?

What characteristics officially qualify a creature for membership in the "Dinosauria"? Dinosaurs cannot be defined by size alone. Some were, in fact, quite small. If they were around today, you'd likely encounter certain varieties at the local pet shop. Dinosaurs are unique among the Mesozoic reptiles in that they were able to walk and run efficiently, not unlike modern mammals and certain flightless birds. Their legs, held vertically beneath the body, gave the early dinosaurs a wider range of movement and fully erect posture, making them faster and more agile than other reptiles, an advantage when competing for food. Their legs could also support great size and weight, something that many genera of dinosaur would eventually attain. Another point to remember is that dinosaurs were land-dwellers. Although there is evidence that individuals may have taken an occasional dip, there were no sea-going dinosaurs. Nor were there any that flew. As a rule of thumb, if the animal had wings or flippers, it wasn't a dinosaur.

The dinosaurs appeared during the Triassic Period and improved on what the thecodonts had begun. The first were generally small meat-eaters, such as *Staurikosaurus* (stor-IK-o-sawr-us) and *Herrerasaurus* (her-RAY-rah-sawr-us), that probably ate any small animals they could catch, including insects and diminutive reptiles. The 8- to 10-foot-long, 300-pound* *Herrerasaurus* was named for an Argentinian guide who led the original expedition to a site that produced the first known remains of this animal. In 1988, fossils of this creature were discovered encased in rock that was between 225 and 230 million years old, making it one of the most ancient dinosaurs uncovered to date.

Your child may ask: How do we know how old rocks are?

There are several ways that geologists determine the age of rocks. One way is to look at the levels of the rock layers. Although layers can sometimes get a little mixed up because of earth movements, basically the oldest rocks are at the bottom.

Another method is called radioactive dating. (No, it's not having lunch at a nuclear plant.) Everything in the universe is made up of atoms. As they age, certain atoms lose little bits from their center. These atoms are known to be radioactive. As this process continues, the radioactive material changes into a nonradioactive material. For example, uranium atoms (radioactive) turn into lead and helium (nonradioactive). This change takes place over a measurable amount of time. By comparing the amount of uranium to lead in uranium-bearing rock, a scientist can estimate how old the rock is.

THE SAURISCHIA

Today, there are about 300 dinosaur genera known, but they did not all coexist. Throughout the Mesozoic Era, some varieties disappeared, and new groups developed to fill the vacated niches. All dinosaurs, however, are divided into two orders according to the shape of their hip bones. *Herrerasaurus* belonged to the Saurischia (saw-RISK-ee-uh), or "lizard-hipped" dinosaurs, which includes plant and meat-eaters alike. Although this group would eventually boast the largest land animals that had ever lived, the *first* saurischians were among the smallest dinosaurs. To

---

*The skeletons of *Herrerasaurus* found thus far seem to have been those of young dinosaurs, in fact, teenagers. University of Chicago evolutionary biologist Paul Sereno calculates that an adult may have been 15 feet long and weighed 600 pounds.

get a better idea of what the saurischians were like, let's take a closer look at the two suborders that make up this group; the Theropoda (thayr-ROP-uh-duh) and the Sauropodomorpha (sawr-uh-pod-uh-MORF-uh).

The Theropoda

The name *Theropoda* means "beast-footed," but most of these animals actually had clawed, birdlike feet with three slender forward-pointing toes, and a dewclaw that pointed backward. They walked on strong hind legs, using their outstretched tails as a counterbalance. Members of this group are generally considered to be meat-eaters, but because of differences in size, diet, and other considerations, they are further divided into two infraorders.

The Carnosauria

The Carnosauria (kar-no-SAWR-ee-uh), or "flesh lizards," are the stuff that monster movies are made of. One of the most notable members, *Tyrannosaurus rex,* may be the only reptile eligible for membership in the Screen Actor's Guild. Because of its great size and astonishing arsenal of daggerlike teeth, one can easily see why people are so dazzled by this dinosaur. *T-rex,* however, may be the best known, but it is not the only one of its ilk. Carnosaurs were all large, heavy-bodied animals with huge skulls, short necks, and impressively long, sharp teeth that continuously fell out and were replaced throughout the animal's life. These beasts were bipedal and, with the exception of one variety, they had short arms. (The latter trait was taken to the extreme by the tyrannosaurids.) As the name implies, carnosaurs dined on flesh. Some were fierce, active hunters, some were probably scavengers, and others may have been opportunists that preferred a fresh kill but would settle for leftovers.

> *With your child: Tyrannosaurus* is the best known, but there were many other carnosaurs that lived during the Mesozoic. Why not put together a file on "dangerous predators of the age"? Categorize them first by time period, then by characteristics. Your list might include *Dilophosaurus,* or "two-crested lizard," which lived during the Early Jurassic Period, and *Megalosaurus, Allosaurus,* and *Ceratosaurus,* among others.

The Coelurosauria

The Coelurosauria (see-loor-oh-SAWR-ee-uh), or "hollow-tailed lizards," were smaller and more lightly built than their larger cousins. A few of their members have been singled out for a number of honors, including the fastest and the most intelligent. Dinosaurs among their ranks range from extremely ferocious predators that prowled in small deadly packs, each pack member equipped with wickedly sharp teeth and claws, to toothless, beaked omnivores as likely to eat fruit as meat. Some coelurosaurs bear a remarkable resemblance to modern birds such as the ostrich, and, in fact, members of this infraorder probably gave rise to the birds. As Yale University paleontologist Dr. John Ostrom points out, "The dinosaurs did not disappear. They simply flew away."

With your child: Make a comparison between the coelurosaurs and modern birds (*Struthiomimus* and the ostrich, for example). First, point out the obvious ways in which they are similar, then focus on the ways in which they are different.

The Sauropodomorpha

It's a little more difficult to generalize about the suborder Sauropodomorpha, or "lizard-footed forms." They were plant-eaters. They ranged in size from about eight feet long to perhaps twice the length of a bowling alley. Some of the smaller species were bipedal, but the giants strolled along on all fours. The sauropodomorphs did share a number of characteristics such as long necks and tails and small heads.

The Prosauropoda

The earliest members of this group belong to the infraorder Prosauropoda (pro-saw-ROP-uh-duh), which means "before sauropods." They turned up in the Late-Triassic Period and, as far as we know, they were among the first true dinosaurs. The most primitive prosauropods were comparatively small and slightly built. In many cases their teeth were suited for eating plants, and they also seemed to have the option of ambling around on four legs or trotting on two. Later prosauropods were decidedly plant-eaters, and the last family to develop included massive, hefty animals that kept all four feet firmly on the ground.

The Sauropoda

If you ask a child to draw a dinosaur, the odds are that he or she will fire off a sketch of a sauropod. The "lizard-footed" members of infra-order Sauropoda (saw-ROP-uh-duh) are the largest, grandest animals that have ever walked this planet. The smallest among them was at least 30 feet long from nose to tail, and the largest may have stretched nearly 130 feet, or almost half a city block long, and weighed 80 to 100 tons! These magnificent giants did not grow to such lengths overnight. Since they had a lifespan of 100 years or more, it's likely that they grew continuously throughout their lives. The sauropods were quadrupedal plant-eaters with pillarlike legs, small skulls (that housed surprisingly small brains), long tails, and long necks. This last characteristic was particularly pronounced in *Mamenchisaurus* (muh-MUN-chee-sawr-us), named for the area in Szechuan Province, China, where its remains were first uncovered. The end of this dinosaur's tail is missing, but scientists estimate that the animal was between 60 and 70 feet long, and half of that length was made up of its neck alone.

Because of their great size, it was once popularly believed that sauropods spent most of their time in water, which supported their ponderous bodies as they grazed on soft aquatic plants. In fact, they were better suited for walking on land and may have traveled across the Mesozoic floodplains in sizable herds. Their long necks were ideal for reaching high into the trees, and patterns of wear on fossil teeth show that these animals regularly ate the twigs and needles of conifers.

Ask your child: How would sauropods benefit from traveling in herds?

Traveling in groups would have been much safer, particularly for young dinosaurs. Fossil trackways show that youngsters generally stayed in the center of the herd, protected by the adults and out of the reach of predators.

THE ORNITHISCHIA

If I haven't touched on the group that includes your child's favorite dinosaur (or yours), don't worry. The four (sometimes five) suborders of the order Ornithischia (or-nih-THISK-ee-uh) include some of the most unusual dinosaurs of all. The name means "bird-hipped," and its was applied because the hip bones of these creatures were similar in arrangement to those of modern birds. Dinosaurs in this group were plant-eaters with hoofed toes. Most had teeth only on the sides of the jaws, and the front of the mouth was modified into a toothless beak.

The Stegosauria

The Stegosauria (steg-oh-SAWR-ee-uh), or "plated lizards," are easily identified by the unusual plates and spikes that adorn their backs and tails. At first glance it seems that these embellishments may have been used as weapons, which is probably true for the tail spikes of the "spiked lizard" *Kentrosaurus* (ken-troh-SAWR-us). The purpose of the plates, however, is not as readily apparent. Scientists have noted that the thin, bony plates were slightly grooved. It's possible that a web of blood vessels was located in these grooves just beneath the skin. The animals could have used the plates as temperature regulators. They would expose the plates to sunlight to warm the blood passing through, or shade them to cool the blood.

There are 11 known kinds of stegosaurs, but *Stegosaurus* (the state fossil of Colorado) is the only member of this suborder that has been found in North America. This slow-moving animal holds the dubious distinction of having the smallest brain compared to body size of any ornithischian.

Your child may ask: How do we know that *Stegosaurus* was slow-moving?

The length of its leg bones and the angle of its body when it walked tell us that this animal moved slowly. The long thigh and short shin are typical of slow-paced animals. Also, because its front legs were much shorter than its hind legs, *Stegosaurus*'s body angled down at the front. This arrangement was not optimum for high speed.

The Ankylosauria

The "armored lizards," members of the Ankylosauria (ang-KY-loh-SAWR-ee-uh), are often and justifiably compared to armored tanks. These well-protected plant-eaters appeared to be very common during the Cretaceous Period, and their remains are found on every continent, including Antarctica. A nest of six wolf-sized baby ankylosaurs was uncovered in the Gobi Desert in 1988.

There were two families of ankylosaurs. The more primitive of the pair, the nodosaurids, were covered by a flexible shield of bony plates set into their tough skin. Spikes that lined the animal's flanks added extra protection against predators that might have attempted to flip it over for a little "ankylosaur on the half shell."

Those of the family Ankylosauridae also had body armor but lacked the flank spikes. Instead, they were equipped with a bony tail club that could probably topple a modern elephant. The most common North American anklyosaurid, *Euoplocephalus* (YU-op-loh-SEF-uh-lus), or "well-armored head," was about 25 feet long, 8 feet wide, and its tail club measured nearly 3 feet across. Both ends of this animal were indeed "well-armored."

> **With your child:** The decline of the stegosaurs was matched by an increase in ankylosaurs. In many ways, these creatures were similar. Compare the two types of animals to see how they each might have filled the same sort of niche. For example, they were both armored herbivores. The stegosaurids and certain ankylosaurids may have employed their tails as weapons.

The Ceratopsia

The Ceratopsia (sayr-uh-TOP-see-uh), the last of the ornithischians to develop, appeared during the Cretaceous Period and enjoyed a mere 20 million years on earth. In that geologically short time the ceratopsians ("horned faces") managed to spread throughout what is now North America and Asia and became extremely abundant in those areas. These animals each sported a neck frill, and their jaw ended in distinct, parrotlike "beaks." Of the three families in this suborder, the "parrot lizards," or Psittacosauridae (SIT-ih-coh-SAWR-ih-dee) were the earliest. They were the only ceratopsians that were mainly bipedal. The frill was not obvious in these animals, but a hint of it was present at the back of the skull.

The neck frill was more pronounced in the family Protoceratopsidae (PRO-to-sayr-uh-TOPS-ih-dee), or "first-horned face," and it bordered on bizarre in some members of the Ceratopsidae (sayr-uh-TOP-sih-dee), the final family to develop. With the exception of one species, the ceratopsids also sprouted from one to three imposing facial horns.

The Ornithopoda

Unlike the ornithischians I've described thus far, the Ornithopoda (or-nih-THOP-uh-duh), or "bird-footed" dinosaurs, were the only group that was essentially "unarmed." Although they lacked armor, clubs, plates, spikes, or horns, they lasted from the Early Jurassic to the Late Cretaceous Period. These plant-eaters routinely walked on two legs but were comfortable browsing slowly on four.

The most varied family was the Hadrosauridae (had-ro-SAWR-ih-dee), the "duck-billed" dinosaurs, named for their wide, flat snouts that looked a little like a duck's bill. The edges were turned down and covered with tough, sharp horn for cropping vegetation, which the animal then ground down on its more than one thousand cheek teeth!

Atop the heads of one subfamily of duckbills grew curious bony crests, some subtle, others wildly flamboyant. What the crests were for is puzzling, but there are a number of ideas to consider. The hollow crests may have been used to amplify sounds the animal made or to enhance the animal's sense of smell. In the case of solid crests, perhaps their shape or color helped the animals to recognize individuals.

The Pachycephalosauria

Some scientists consider the highly specialized "dome-headed" dinosaurs, the Pachycephalosauria (PAK-ee-sef-uh-loh-SAWR-ee-uh), to be a unique group of ornithopods. Some place it in a suborder of its own. These unusual animals definitely seem like the "odd dinosaurs out" when compared with others of their kind. Although the shapes or sizes were different depending on the genera, pachycephalosaurs were equipped with what has come to be called the "dinosaur crash helmet." Also known as "boneheads," these creatures had extremely thick skulls often surrounded by a wreath of bony knobs. Scientists speculate that the headgear was useful in "butting contests" among males. These dinosaurs may have been mountain-dwellers with lifestyles similar to that of modern mountain goats.

A QUESTION OF DEGREE

An introduction to the dinosaurs would not be complete without touching on this question: Were they warm-blooded or cold-blooded? The answer is at the very heart of our perception of the dinosaurs as vigorous and energetic. Warm-bloodedness would set them even farther apart from their reptile relatives.

Scientists who first studied dinosaurs found them similar to modern reptiles in that both appeared to have comparable claws, scaly skin, and uniformly shaped teeth. For decades, paleontologists assumed that dinosaurs, like modern reptiles, were also cold-blooded. Since the 1960s, that assumption has been constantly put to the test.

First, we need to look at modern warm-blooded and cold-blooded creatures. Any animal runs and hunts best when its body is evenly warmed. The body temperature of birds and animals, such as humans, is controlled by internal processes. When we "burn" the food we eat, we produce body heat. About nine-tenths of our food is utilized just to keep us warm, day or night. To get rid of excess heat, mammals may increase blood flow to the surface of the skin.

Ask your child: What are some other ways that mammals can get rid of excess heat?

They may pant or sweat.

Most modern reptiles bask in direct sunlight to warm themselves to an ideal body temperature. They don't sweat or pant as mammals do when they get too hot. Instead, a reptile finds shade or perhaps cools off in water if it is available. If a reptile's body temperature is less than optimum, the creature's running speed decreases, and the time it takes to digest a meal increases. The animal becomes sluggish.

Now consider the case for warm-blooded dinosaurs on behavior alone. Perhaps, these animals were not slow and sluggish. Although the basic hunting tactic of modern reptiles is to ambush prey while expending as little effort as possible, some meat-eating dinosaurs appear to have stalked prey for long distances or engaged in battles that required a tremendous output of energy. Many were able to sprint at fairly high speeds for short distances.

The discovery of the remains of Cretaceous dinosaurs in areas that were within the Arctic and Antarctic circles when the animals were alive raises other questions. Granted, the climate was warmer then, but how would these dinosaurs have coped with the polar night? Warm-blooded animals could certainly have fared better than cold-blooded ones. The dinosaurs may have migrated for hundreds of miles or more on a seasonal basis, as modern mammals and birds do.

With your child: To demonstrate that the polar regions spend a lot of time in twilight or darkness, place a lamp in the center of the room. If you can remove the lamp shade the effect will be more obvious. You will also need an apple and a knitting needle. Push the needle through the bottom of the apple and out the top. The apple is the earth, the knitting needle is the axis, and the lamp is the sun. The top of the apple is the northern polar region and the bottom is the southern polar region. Have your child grasp the lower end of the needle and tilt the "earth" to about 23 degrees. Now he or she must walk around the sun once without changing the tilt or angle of the earth. Note that the northern polar region is in light and darkness for equal amounts of time. The same thing happens as the real earth moves in its yearly journey around the sun.

Behavior alone does not provide an adequate answer to the warm-blooded/cold-blooded question, and unfortunately, there are few physical clues. It would be easier to solve if the dinosaurs' internal organs, which are more complex in warm-blooded animals, had not decayed and had been fossilized along with their bones. Still, some clues survive in the bones. By analyzing bone size and structure, scientists show that many dinosaurs were designed for speed and agility. The internal structure of their bones also hints at endothermy in some dinosaurs. When viewed in cross-section, dinosaur bones seem to compare more favorably with mammal bones than with those of modern reptiles in both form and deduced growth rate.

Accepting that some dinosaurs may have been warm-blooded, however, is not an all-or-nothing choice. You could call it a matter of degree. Mammals generally operate at an internal temperature ranging from 97 to 106 degrees F. It's possible that dinosaurs managed quite well over a different range of body temperatures. Even the internal temperature of some mammals varies widely at times. In addition, body size is a major factor in the way that an animal gains or loses heat. Body heat is lost to the environment via the creature's surface area. The greater the volume of a beast's body compared to its surface area, the better it retains heat. An elephant, for example, retains heat better than a chipmunk. A huge dinosaur like *Apatosaurus* would naturally retain heat better than a small animal. The large dinosaurs may not have needed to be warm-blooded. Even so, the evidence in favor of at least some warm-blooded dinosaurs is mounting.

With your child: Here's a simple way to show that a large body retains heat more readily than a small one. You will need a thermometer and two different-sized glass jars that have similar shapes (a half-pint and a quart canning jar will work well). Fill both jars with very hot water and take the temperature of each. Put caps on the jars and set them on a countertop away from drafts. Return every 10 minutes or so to record their temperatures again. You will see that the larger jar takes much longer to cool down. That is because its surface-to-volume ratio is smaller than that of the small jar. The same principle may have enabled large dinosaurs to keep their body temperatures steady.

2

What Is Not a Dinosaur?

Simply living during the Mesozoic Era did not qualify a reptile as a dinosaur. Dinosaurs shared their world with many extraordinary creatures. The lord of the Mesozoic skies, for example, was the pterosaur (TAYR-oh-sawr). Neither prehistoric birds nor bats, and not the ancestors of either, pterosaurs were actually "winged reptiles."

REPTILES IN THE AIR

Roughly 80 varieties of pterosaur filled some of the niches occupied today by modern birds. All were lightly built and flew on leathery wings of skin that were supported by their incredibly long fourth fingers and stretched from shoulder to thigh. Most had large eyes and probably excellent eyesight, an advantage for an animal that may have cruised above the surface of inland seas looking for a fish dinner. Like small, active dinosaurs, the pterosaurs may have been warm-blooded, and at least one variety, it seems, developed a way to retain body heat. There is no evidence of feathered pterosaurs, but in 1971, a Soviet scientist found several well-preserved fossils. Although its tail was bare, one of the specimens exhibited evidence of a shaggy, two-inch-long covering of hair on its wings and small body. The scientist dubbed this little creature *Sordes pilosus* (SOR-deez py-LO-sus), or "hairy devil."

Your child may ask: Did other pterosaurs have a furry coat?

That question hasn't been settled. In fact, each fossil discovery suggests more questions than answers about these unusual animals. Were they capable of powered flight, or did they simply glide from place to place? How did they launch themselves into the air? Could they maneuver comfortably on the ground, or were they clumsy as are modern bats? The answers to these questions may be different for each type of pterosaur.

The order Pterosauria is divided into two suborders. The Rhamphorhynchoidea (RAM-foh-rink-OY-dee-uh), or "prow beaks," developed during the Late Triassic Period and continued to soar through the skies well into the Jurassic Period. These sparrow- to hawk-sized animals had short necks and long tails often tipped with a small kite-shaped blade of bone at the end, which may have served as a rudder.

Eudimorphodon (yoo-dy-MORF-uh-don), which means "true two-form tooth," had broad teeth at the rear of its short jaws, and peglike teeth at the front. It was about two feet long, but half of that length was in its slim, bony tail. The first three fingers of each hand ended in sharp claws, and the long fourth fingers supported the leading edge of its wings. This animal had a broad, flattened breastbone that may have anchored flight muscles. Some researchers think that *Eudimorphodon* may have been an active flier.

Dimorphodon (dy-MORF-uh-don), or "two-form tooth," had a wingspan of four feet across and was about the size of a large hawk. Its huge head accounted for one-quarter of its entire body length and gave it a general appearance somewhat like a prehistoric puffin. *Dimorphodon* may have been exceptional in another way as well. According to the structure of its hips and legs, this rhamphorhynchoid may have been able to walk gracefully on land, like a modern bird.

Your child may ask: Why did different pterosaurs have different-shaped beaks?

The beaks were adapted to the type of food that the animal ate. The same is true for modern birds. Look at the sharp, curved beak of a flesh-eating eagle, the long, slender beak of a hummingbird, or the short, stout beak of a seed-eating sparrow. If you're at the zoo or on a nature hike and see birds feeding, note the shape of the beak and what type of food the birds are eating. See if you can see a pattern.

The rhamphorhynchoids disappeared toward the end of the Jurassic Period. From that point until the close of the Mesozoic Era, members of the suborder Pterodactyloidea (TAYR-uh-dak-til-OY-dee-uh) reigned supreme in the air. They had long, slender necks but only a stub of a tail or none at all. Their name means "wing fingers" and, as with all pterosaurs, their long fourth fingers supported slender wing membranes. This suborder produced a wonderful array of intriguing animals that lend credence to the saying "truth is stranger than fiction." *Pterodaustro* (tayr-uh-DAWS-tro), which means "southern wing," had a bizarre set of teeth lining its curved lower jaw. These teeth grew long, thin, and very close together to form a kind of sieve. *Pterodaustro* probably fed on plankton. By flying just above the surface of the sea and dragging its open mouth through the water, it could collect a meal in this special trap.

With your child: The modern flamingo has filtering bristles and probably feeds somewhat like *Pterodaustro* once did. There is a big difference, however, because the filtering bristles of the flamingo are in its upper jaw, while those of *Pterodaustro* were in its lower jaw. On your next trip to the zoo, pay a visit to the flamingos to see how they use their unusual beaks.

The first pterodactyls were pigeon-sized, but it seems that nature had no intention of stopping there. *Pteranodon* (tayr-AN-uh-don), or "winged and toothless" (correct on both counts), was about the size of a large goose, but it had a wingspan of nearly 27 feet. In spite of its size, this animal weighed no more than 30 or 40 pounds. Because of its long beak and a slim crest that swept back from its skull, *Pteranodon*'s head measured 6 feet from end to end. Like other pterosaurs, this animal, too, fed on fish, scooping them from the sea in its toothless beak.

Your child may ask: What was the crest of *Pteranodon* used for?
The purpose of the crest is a mystery, but it has been suggested that it was used as a stabilizer in flight to offset the animal's long beak.

Quetzalcoatlus (KET-zal-koh-AT-lus), the largest of the pterosaurs, was named after Quetzalcoatl, a fabled feathered serpent-god. This animal cruised the inland skies over what is now North America. It may have been a scavenger, riding on warm air currents to survey the land below, then spiraling downward to tear at the carcass of a fallen dinosaur. A denizen of the Late Cretaceous Period, *Quetzalcoatlus* was undoubtedly the largest flying creature ever to have lived. This reptile weighed up to 140 pounds, had a 10-foot-long snakelike neck, and the wingspan of nearly 40 feet across—almost that of a small twin-engine aircraft! But at the end of the Mesozoic Era, all of the pterosaurs, this mighty giant included, disappeared forever.

Your child may ask: How was this animal able to ride air currents?

Warm air rises. The surface of the land is usually heated unevenly and creates "hot spots." The warm air over these spots moves upward in a swiftly rising column, and *Quetzalcoatlus* was able to hitch a ride on this current of air.

Archaeopteryx

One of the world's most valuable fossils was unearthed in 1861 in a German limestone quarry. At first it was thought to be the remains of a tiny Jurassic dinosaur. On closer examination, scientists discovered that the creature was surrounded by clear impressions of feathers! It wasn't a feathered dinosaur or pterosaur, but rather a primitive 150-million-year-old bird. Crow-sized *Archaeopteryx* (ar-kee-OP-ter-iks), or "ancient wing," was an incredible link between reptiles and birds, and convincing evidence that bolstered the theory of evolution. There is no doubt about *Archaeopteryx*'s reptilian roots. It had many characteristics common to small dinosaurs, including a long, bony tail, small, sharp teeth, long legs designed for running, and three small clawed fingers that extended from the leading edge of its wing.

In addition, *Archaeopteryx* had a fused collarbone, or wishbone, as all birds do. This little animal probably took to the air in short leaps and glides because it lacked the keeled breastbone that enables birds to fly long distances. Its hind claws were straighter than those of perching birds, so paleontologists aren't certain whether it lived in the trees or spent most of its time on the ground. What distinguishes this creature, however, is that it had a covering of feathers, a characteristic exclusive to birds. Still, *Archaeopteryx,* the only member of the suborder Archaeornithes (ar-kee-YOR-nih-theez), or "ancient bird," is not necessarily the ancestor of, or even directly related to, modern birds. It's more likely that this animal and the birds developed from a common ancestor.

Scientists disagree as to the use of *Archaeopteryx*'s feathers. Some believe they were for thermal control since *Archaeopteryx* was probably warm-blooded. Another hypothesis is that the feathers served as a kind of net to trap flying insects. Some of the feathers, however, are similar in form to the flight feathers of modern birds, so one contingent suggests that this prehistoric bird was capable of powered flight.

Your child may ask: How were the feathers of *Archaeopteryx* similar to the feathers of modern birds?

The flight features of modern birds are asymmetrical. That means that the feather is wider on one side of the central shaft than on the other. This seems to aid in flight. *Archaeopteryx,* too, had asymmetrical feathers.

REPTILES IN THE SEA

There is plenty of evidence that dinosaurs could and did swim, but most were confirmed land-dwellers. Some reptiles, however, returned to the sea and eventually dominated the marine world. The largest, most successful, and perhaps the most widely known are of the order Plesiosauria (plee-zee-oh-SAWR-ee-uh), or "near lizards." These beasts cut gracefully through the water in search of a meal that may have consisted of fish or other reptiles. Strong swimmers, they propelled themselves forward by moving their flippers in strokes much like the flying motion of a bird's wing. When the time came to lay their eggs, the plesiosaurs may have used their flippers to drag themselves onto shore. Modern marine turtles also display this breeding behavior.

Ask your child: Why did this animal have to lay its eggs on land?

Air must get inside the eggs of an air-breathing animal or the young will die.

The plesiosaurs were divided into two superfamilies that differed in their feeding habits and the size of their heads and necks. The "thin-plated lizard," *Elasmosaurus* (ee-LAZ-moh-sawr-us), belonged to the long-necked Superfamily Plesiosauridea. Its flexible neck accounted for half of the animal's 45-foot length. *Elasmosaurus* probably swam slowly at the ocean's surface with its neck arched high out of the water. When it spotted its unwary prey, it would fling its head forward and strike, grasping the victim with its sharply pointed teeth.

The fierce, maneuverable Pliosauridea (ply-oh-SAWR-ih-dee-uh), or "more lizards," were the terrors of the Mesozoic oceans. The largest among them, *Kronosaurus* (KROH-noh-sawr-us), was named for Kronos, the Greek god of time. At 42 feet long it was the largest of the short-necked plesiosaurs, and one-quarter of that length was made up of its massive skull. This giant's terrifying, eight-foot-long, dagger-toothed jaws enabled it to rip apart very large prey, or swallow smaller prey whole.

The Ichthyosaurs

The prehistoric waters were filled with danger and, in the animal world, a time-honored method of survival has always been the ability to beat a hasty retreat. The Ichthyosauria (ik-thee-oh-SAWR-ee-uh), which means "fish lizards," were the fastest marine reptiles. With the exception of a vertical orientation of the tail, some looked much like modern dolphins, complete with a stabilizing dorsal fin rising from a gently arched back. Ichthyosaurs, streamlined and built for speed, may have cut through the water at 20 or 30 miles per hour. They swam by powerful side-to-side strokes of the tail and used their paired fins to steer. Like dolphins today, these creatures were air-breathers and had to surface regularly.

The ichthyosaurs, however, were completely adapted to life in the warm sea. They represent one of the few reptile groups that are confirmed to have given live birth. In fact, one German fossil specimen actually shows such a birth in process! As the young ichthyosaur was entering the world, tail first, some disaster prevented the tiny reptile from ever drawing its first breath, and stilled its laboring mother as well.

Your child may ask: If ichthyosaurs and dolphins aren't related, why do they look so much alike?

They look alike because these unrelated ocean-dwellers adapted to their watery surroundings in similar ways. Both relied on speed to escape predators and capture food, and both developed such characteristics as a streamlined body and a powerful, muscular tail that helped them to swim quickly.

Ask your child: What do you think is one reason that ichthyosaurs developed live birth?

They would have been helpless if they had to drag themselves onto land to lay eggs. By giving live birth, they didn't have to leave the water.

The Mosasaurs

In spite of their names, none of the Mesozoic animals mentioned thus far were actually lizards, but marine lizards did in fact ply the waters of the Mesozoic, and some were very fierce indeed. Named for the Meuse River in Holland where their remains were first discovered, the Mosasauridae (moh-za-SAWR-ih-dee) were closely related to modern monitor lizards (the most famous of which is the 10-foot-long, 300-pound Komodo Dragon of Indonesia). One huge representative of the family was *Plotosaurus* (plawt-oh-SAWR-us). Its jaws were armed with sharp teeth, and its enormous 30-foot-long body was powered through the sea by an incredibly strong, flat tail. These efficient predators probably ate fish, squid, ammonites (a kind of shellfish), reptiles, and sea birds. The Cretaceous mosasaurs of North America's shallow central sea, the Niobrara, reached 40 feet in length. They were surpassed by Belgian beasts that have been estimated at lengths of more than 50 feet.

Your child may ask: Are there any sea-going lizards living now?

Yes. The marine iguana. This lizard of the Galapagos Islands suns itself on the rocky island shores and dives into the sea to feed on algae. The marine iguana may measure more than four feet in length.

Mammallike Reptiles

One of the most common cases of mistaken identity is that of *Dimetrodon* (dy-MEE-troh-don), the largest meat-eater of the Permian Period. Years ago, this sail-backed critter commonly made its way into popular film and print as some sort of dinosaur. Guess again. Not only did this reptile live millions of years before the first dinosaur trod the earth, it was a member of a group that would eventually produce our very own ancestors.

Ask your child: Many people mistake this creature for a dinosaur. What is one feature you can see that tells you that *Dimetrodon* was not a dinosaur?

Dimetrodon had a sprawling stance characteristic of early reptiles, not dinosaurs.

As the Paleozoic Era drew to a close, the great swamps were replaced by dry forests of pine and fir, and arid deserts stretched far inland. With their watertight skin and shelled eggs, small, early reptiles prospered in this new world. Among them were the subclass Synapsida (sih-NAP-sid-uh), the mammallike reptiles. At first glance it isn't easy to distinguish between these creatures and their other reptilian neighbors, and the similarities between them and today's mammals are even less obvious. The earliest reptiles (and amphibians as well) have no openings in their skulls other than those for the eyes and nostrils. These animals are called *anapsids. Diapsids,* which include dinosaurs and other archosaurs, had a pair of openings in the skull behind the eye. The *synapsids,* however, had only one opening behind the eye.

Dimetrodon, meaning "two-measure teeth," belonged to the "basin lizards," or Order Pelycosauria (pel-EE-koh-SAWR-ee-uh), a very early form of synapsid. Like other reptiles, *Dimetrodon* was cold-blooded but had an innovative way of warming itself. A "sail" of leathery skin on its back, supported by spines more than three feet long at the center, was probably laced with blood vessels. This novel sail helped *Dimetrodon* to regulate its body temperature. By turning its sail to absorb the rays of the early morning sun, the predator could cut its "warm-up" time by more than two-thirds, thus gaining an extra advantage over its prey.

Dimetrodon had another trait that qualified it as a mammallike reptile. Its powerful jaws were lined with two kinds of teeth: shearing teeth as well as several canine teeth for stabbing.

> ***Ask your child:*** We are mammals. How many different types of teeth do we have and what are they used for?
>
> We have four kinds of teeth for cutting, stabbing, slicing, and grinding. Encourage your youngster to look in the mirror and see for himself or herself.

Therapsids

The Therapsida (ther-RAP-sid-uh), for "beast opening," were highly advanced synapsids, and their remains have been found throughout the world. The most successful of these were of the suborder Cynodontia (sih-noh-DONT-ee-uh), or "dog toothed."

CHAPTER

3

The Mesozoic Era

Dinosaurs have been depicted in such diverse environments as sun-baked, crimson-sand deserts, lush, steamy swamps, and windswept floodplains dotted with shallow ponds. Some scenes also include volcanoes spewing out fountains of lava. All these descriptions are actually correct depending on the animals represented.

With your child: You and your youngster might enjoy this game. Up to four can play. Draw or cut out four different scenes from a nature magazine. You can include an underwater reef, a mountain meadow, a desert, a shoreline, or perhaps a forest. Now cut out or draw ten pictures of animals for each scene. You should have 40 pictures. Mix up the pictures and place them in a shoe box. Each player chooses a scene and takes a turn drawing an animal picture from the shoe box. If the animal "fits" the scene the player keeps the picture. If not, the picture goes back into the box. Continue playing until someone has matched up all ten animals that belong in his or her environment.

Of course, animals have changed quite a bit since the days of the dinosaurs. From its infancy, our dynamic Earth has always been subject to change on a grand scale. Five billion years ago, the seeds of this planet, bits of rock and dust, gathered into an ever-growing sphere that whirled in orbit around our violent young sun. The cold, lifeless protoplanet swept up everything in its path. Gravitational compression, radioactivity, and constant meteoroid bombardment eventually heated Earth to a bubbling, fiery mass with a consistency resembling taffy. After millions of years, the seething surface cooled enough to form a hard crust over the molten interior. Gases, cooked from the smoldering rocks, created a primitive atmosphere. Water vapor fell back to Earth as rain, forming globe-girdling oceans in which the first simple, single-celled lifeforms appeared. It took several billion years for the first vertebrate life to climb out of the warm seas to claim the garden planet for its own.

Scientists have divided Earth's entire history into four eras. The first era, the Precambrian, covers a tremendous span of time from the birth of the planet some 4.6 billion years ago to about 590 million years ago. Life during that period was simple and limited to the sea.

The Paleozoic Era, which means era of "ancient life," followed. This era lasted for about 340 million years and saw the development of a myriad of new plant forms, from the first green and red algae in the sea to gigantic conifers and tree ferns on land. Animal life expanded from soft-bodied marine creatures to mighty beasts such as *Dimetrodon.* The Mesozoic Era for "middle life," is known mainly for the reign of the dinosaurs, but by its end, every major class of animals on Earth, including mammals, was represented in one form or another. A global mass extinction about 65 million years ago brought the Mesozoic Era to an end.*

Your child may ask: What is extinction?

When an animal species is extinct, there are no living representatives left on Earth. The species is gone forever. The dodo bird and the passenger pigeon are animals that have become extinct in modern times.

A great deal of attention has been given to determining what caused the extinction of the dinosaurs (see chapter 6), but the Mesozoic Era also *began* in the wake of one of the most severe mass extinctions in Earth's history—the Permian crisis—which occurred roughly between 255 and 250 MYA. About 75 to 90 percent of preexisting species, half of all the families that populated the seas, were eliminated. Entire classes of animals were left with only a few representatives. It was not a rapid extinction; rather, it was a great dying that spread over several millions of years. Some families succumbed much earlier than others. New groups evolved to take their place, then also perished. Terrestrial life was not spared either. Varieties of mammallike reptiles, for example, disappeared

---

*The latest segment of geologic time, our own, is the Cenozoic, for "recent life." One may not want to speculate about what may bring this era to a close, but the human species is the first capable of knowingly contributing to, or avoiding, its own demise.

in what seemed to be a close series of extinctions which particularly affected large animals. The Permian crisis was probably caused by a climatic shift—a cooling trend to which these animals could not adapt. Of the creatures that remained, both the thecodonts and the therapsids had produced forms that were capable and efficient, but the tide swung in favor of the descendants of the thecodonts, and the Mesozoic Era earned the name "the age of the dinosaurs."

Ask your child: Can you think of any animals that are in danger of becoming extinct today?

The California condor, the white rhino, the Siberian tiger, and the blue whale are considered endangered species.

THE TRIASSIC PERIOD

Scientists have divided the Mesozoic into three parts, or periods. The first temporal slice, the Triassic Period, lasted from 248 MYA to 208 MYA. It is named for three layers of rock that formed at the time in what is now central Germany—a layer of marine origin sandwiched between two tiers of nonmarine rock.

If you could travel back in time to the dawn of the Triassic Period, you would find a completely alien world. The continents we know today were then gathered into a single megacontinent called Pangaea (pan-GEE-uh), or "all Earth," surrounded by Panthalassa, "all sea," which covered more than half the globe. It would have been possible to walk from North America to Africa, or from Antarctica to Australia, without getting your feet wet. There were no huge caps of ice glistening at the poles. Mighty mountains that now seem so eternal—the Alps, Andes, Himalayas, and Rockies—did not exist, though there were other ranges that have since worn away.

With your child: Several million years ago, the Appalachians in the eastern United States were huge towering mountains. Visit the library and try to find photographs of the Appalachians as they look today and discuss the power of erosion with your child. Ask what forces might help to wear mountains away.

At least it would be easy to pack for such a trip. The warm, dry climate changed little with the seasons. For thousands of miles, sand dunes stretched across huge inland deserts. Warm, salt lakes were scattered about, and occasional rains created freshwater pools fringed by ferns and cycads. Tall conifers, similar to modern pines, fared well in drier soil. A tremendous gulf known as the Tethys Sea intruded deeply into the continent. The modern Mediterranean Sea is a remnant of this ancient waterway. Along its shores, shallow lagoons crowded with life covered much of what is now southern Europe. And toward the end of the period, England languished under muddy seas.

With your child: If you can find a photograph of the White Cliffs of Dover at your local library or bookstore, show it to your youngster. Explain that those cliffs were once underwater and were formed from the shells of ancient sea creatures.

The wake of the Permian crisis created tremendous opportunity for animals that survived. The primitive ancestors of the dinosaurs were able to expand their ranges and fill empty niches, but at the end of the Triassic there was another great dying. Although the event is poorly understood because of a lack of fossil evidence, it seems that the blow came in the form of a one-two punch. First, the earliest amphibians and, with the exception of one family, the mammallike reptiles disappeared. The thecodont group, too, was hit hard. A second wave seemed to focus on the sea. Families of marine invertebrates that had held on through the beginning of the era finally slipped away. Ichthyosaurs appear to have been the only large marine reptiles to survive the calamity. On land, the theocodonts finally slipped into extinction.

Generally, this upheaval is thought to have been the result of changes in climate and a rise in sea level. Some scientists point to the 212-million-year-old, 62-mile-wide Manicouagan Crater in Quebec, as the site of an asteriod impact that may have added to those problems.

THE JURASSIC PERIOD

The second period was the Jurassic (jewr-AS-ik), named for rock strata discovered in the Swiss-French Jura Mountains. The strata was deposited between 208 and 144 MYA. At that time, the supercontinent, shaken by earthquakes and volcanic activity, was preparing to wrench itself apart at the western edge of the Tethys Sea. The waters slowly pulsed back and forth across the lowlands, draining some areas and flooding others, then reversing the process. Ancient coral polyps built huge reefs around islands that studded the Tethys, creating clear, shallow lagoons where pterosaurs hunted for fish and perhaps squid. Today the Black Forest of southern Germany stands where waves once licked those island shores.

Although hot, dry conditions persisted in some areas, the encroaching sea generally brought moisture and a more moderate climate. Swamps, lush and green with horsetails, seed ferns and towering tree ferns, extended along the coasts and far inland. Because of the milder conditions, even in dry areas, fern-dotted plains replaced deserts. Vegetation was more plentiful over a much wider range than before, and the Jurassic Period became a time of giants. Colossal sauropods browsed among the trees, while immense meat-eaters stalked their prey.

> *With your child:* During the Jurassic Period, conifers were very common, and they are still common today. There may even be some in your neighborhood. Here are hints on how to recognize the three main kinds of conifers and tell the differences among them. Conifers are evergreens. Their long, thin leaves are called needles. They lose their needles but not all at once; rather, the leaves drop all year round so it isn't as noticeable. The needles of the pine tree grow in long, slender bunches. Spruce trees have sharp, pointed needles that are four-sided. The needles found on fir trees are short and not sharp. When you pluck a fir needle, you can see the spot on the branch where the needle was.

The weather was also more changeable during the Jurassic than it had been in earlier periods. Rain and flooding were followed by dry spells during which many varieties of dinosaur migrated great distances in search of food. They could no longer wander at will, however. Widening seas and obstacles similar to the Great Rift Valley of East Africa blocked passage. By the mid-Jurassic, a nascent North Atlantic Ocean had parted North America and Africa and had begun to split North America from Europe.

For a time, a formidable river about a thousand miles long flowed from the highlands of North America to the West, where it emptied into the waters of Panthalassa. The highlands themselves (precursors of today's Rocky Mountains) formed a long, slender peninsula. On the ocean side, volcanic islands collided like slow-motion bumper cars into the coast. To the East, the Sundance Sea, an arm of the Arctic Ocean, invaded deeply into the continent. It covered what is today the Great Plains and much of the land that would eventually rest atop the slopes of the present Rocky Mountains. Sediments washed from the highlands built up along the borders of the Sundance Sea, creating a strip of fertile floodplains from Montana to New Mexico. Such areas were ideal for the preservation of fossils, and indeed, this area, known today as the Morrison Formation, yields some of North America's finest nonmarine Jurassic fossils. Many of the creatures discovered there represent families and species that did not survive the close of the Jurassic Period. With the exception of those isolated in China and India, the stegosaurs died out. And although a few varieties endured, the footsteps of many of the great sauropods faded as well.

Your child may ask: What caused the continent of Pangaea to split apart?

Disturbances in the Earth's mantle beneath the crust can cause the land to split and form a rift. One way this happens is if molten rock, called magma, pushes up toward the surface. It forms a bulge and eventually the land on either side of the bulge splits and fractures. Molten rock from below oozes upward into the rift. It ultimately hardens and forms new crust. The sides of the rift are pushed further apart to make room. Eventually sea water fills the opening and the continent is finally split. The same process is occurring today in East Africa in a place called the Great Rift Valley.

THE CRETACEOUS PERIOD

The final period of the Mesozoic Era, the Cretaceous (kree-TAY-shee-us), lasted from about 145 and 65 MYA. *Creta* is Latin for "chalk," and throughout Europe, chalk was the predominant rock produced during the period. A prime example of a Cretaceous formation is the White Cliffs of Dover.

This was a time of sweeping change. The supercontinent no longer existed. Its southern segment, known as Gondwanaland (try saying that with a straight face) had splintered into South America, Africa, and large fragments that would eventually break up to form Antarctica as well as Australia, India, and Madagascar.

Much of Europe gained a temporary respite from the sea as the waters withdrew. In their wake, freshwater lakes appeared. Extending from England to Germany, Wealden Lake was the final resting place of many Early Cretaceous dinosaurs. Fossils preserved in its sediments include remains of *Iguanodon* and *Hypsilophodon,* among the first creatures to be recognized as dinosaurs. Herds of *Iguanodon* probably grazed on the abundant vegetation that flourished along the lakeshore, while carnivores prowling nearby sought to make a meal of a straggler from the herd.

As the period progressed, Mother Nature introduced one of her most remarkable innovations—flowering plants. These were able to reproduce more quickly and under a wider range of circumstances than most other forms of plants and so had a distinct advantage. Ferns and conifers were generally replaced by hardwood trees such as oak and hickory, and ivory-petaled magnolias were widespread. (It would be well into the Cenozoic Era, however, before Earth's great grasslands appeared.)

Ask your child: What are some ways in which seeds can travel and thus populate new areas?

They can travel by wind; water; they can stick to animal skin or fur and be carried from place to place; they can be eaten by an animal, pass through the creature's system, and be deposited many miles from the parent plant.

By the end of the Cretaceous, Australia clung to Antarctica by a thread, while Greenland still nestled close to Scandinavia, but the modern continents were largely defined. As the Atlantic and Indian oceans widened, Panthalassa no longer merited the name "all sea," although even today its heir, the Pacific Ocean, is still the largest. The sea level rose globally to its highest levels (most of Europe was again submerged) and climates varied in different parts of the world.

With your child: Study the modern continents on a globe. Are there any that look like they would fit well together?

North Africa was warm and dry, but not arid. In fact, the area seems to have been heavily foliated and subject to seasonal rain. Below the sands of the modern Sahara are the remains of swamps that were once home to crocodiles, early snakes, and turtles. Even in the semidesert of Mongolia, life prospered around freshwater lakes and springs. This was the territory of a mysterious creature that has been identified only by its front limbs and a few ribs, enough to indicate it was a fearsome predator. The arms of *Deinocheirus* (dy-noh-KY-rus), or "terrible hand," measured nine feet in length, and each claw is up to a foot long. In life, when covered by horny sheaths, these claws would have been longer. But the most impressive claws belong to *Therezinosaurus* (THER-ih-zin-oh-SAWR-us), for "scythe lizard," a beast that stalked the same desert and was equipped with claws nearly a yard long!

With your child: Have your child draw a picture of what Deinocheirus might have looked like.

The most notorious predator of the Cretaceous, *Tyrannosaurus rex,* was a denizen of North America—or what there was of it. One-third of the continent, much of Canada and the central and southeastern United States, were all underwater. An ancient reef formed where Chicago presently stands, and mosasaurs, monstrous turtles, and 20-foot-long sharks swam over what is now known as the grain belt. The Niobrara Sea filled the area that during the Jurassic Period had been inundated by the Sundance Sea. The Niobrara, however, extended from the Arctic to the Gulf of Mexico, effectively cutting the continent in two. Some regions of the modern central plains are buried under a layer of marine sediment nearly a mile deep! (The likenesses of the presidents on Mount Rushmore give us not only a view of human history but a rare glimpse of the granite foundation of our prehistoric continent.)

Your child may ask: Are the present conditions changing still?
    Yes, the plates on which the continents rest are still moving. Some are shifting as much as several inches each year.

MESOZOIC NEIGHBORS

Many of the animals that shared the dinosaur's world would appear quite familiar to us today. Examples of some of these creatures are as near as your backyard. Two-thirds of all modern insects developed before or during the Mesozoic Era. Wasps, bees, dragonflies, butterflies, and moths buzzed or fluttered in the air. Beetles skittered across the ground, and huge cockroaches skulked among the leaf litter (obviously waiting for the development of the modern kitchen cupboard). The dinosaurs were probably annoyed by flies and perhaps even fleas.

Ask your child: Insects played a very important role during the Mesozoic. Can you think of two things that they did?
    Insects were a source of food for small dinosaurs and other reptiles. They also pollinated the flowering plants of the Cretaceous Period.

Lizards and Snakes

Many vertebrate forms made their debut in the Mesozoic. Snakes and lizards belong to the order Squamata. Land-dwelling lizards first appeared during the Late Permian Era and evolved side-by-side with the dinosaurs. Some primitive varieties developed unique traits to aid in capturing their prey and to avoid ending up as a snack for their ubiquitous cousins. By staying in the trees, *Kuehneosaurus* (cue-nee-oh-SAWR-us) could safely hunt for its own food. The ribs of this primitive Triassic lizard extended outward on each side and supported a sheet of tough skin. The creature was able to spread these membranous wings to a span of about one foot and used them to glide through the air from tree to tree. The kuehneosaurids have no living representatives, but the family that includes modern geckos can be traced directly to a group that appeared during the Jurassic Period.

There isn't a very good fossil record of ancient snakes, but there is some sketchy evidence that they appeared in the Cretaceous Period. They may have originally developed from burrowing lizards or perhaps from an aquatic lizard such as *Pachyrhachis* (pak-ee-RA-kis). Some modern snakes have signs of a hip bone that would only have been needed by a creature that had legs at some point in its evolution. Found in Argentina, the oldest fossil serpents seem related to the family that includes pythons and boas. *Dinilysia* (dy-neh-LEE-zia), or "terrible destroyer," was probably a constrictor. It had developed the wide gape characteristic of modern snakes, and it's likely that *Dinilysia* fed on small mammals, lizards, insects . . . maybe even young dinosaurs.

Your child may ask: Were there any poisonous snakes during the Mesozoic Period?

No. Poisonous snakes did not develop until well into the Tertiary Period.

Turtles, Tortoises, and Terrapins

Turtles, tortoises, and terrapins make up the order Chelonia. *Proganochelys* (proh-gan-oh-KEL-ees) means "first turtle," and this yard-long land-dweller made its first appearance in the Triassic Period. It was fitted with an armored shell and a sharp-edged beak like those of a modern turtle. Although it couldn't pull in its head and legs, *Proganochelys*'s shell was trimmed with flat plates that extended out to protect the legs, and its neck was studded with bony spikes.

The largest turtle that ever lived, *Archelon* (ARK-ee-lon) was 12 feet long and 11 feet wide. It belonged to a family of spectacular sea turtles that cruised through the waters of the Niobrara Sea during the Cretaceous Period. Rather than the clawed feet and heavy horn-covered carapace of its terrestrial relatives, it had paddlelike flippers and was covered by a protective shield of tough, rubbery skin.

Ask your child: Not counting size, what modern turtle seems most like *Archelon*?

The leatherback turtle is also a sea-going turtle with paddlelike flippers and a leathery shell.

The Crocodiles

Have you ever wondered what a crocodile is smiling about? Perhaps it is because members of the order Crocodylia are the only archosaurs to have survived, virtually unchanged, to present times. As with most aquatic and semiaquatic reptiles, the order began with terrestrial animals. During the mid-Triassic, *Gracilisuchus* (gruh-sill-ih-SOOK-us) showed links to the thecondonts that preceded it and to the crocodiles that would follow it. Only a foot long, *Gracilisuchus* was a lightly built land-dweller that ran skillfully on its hind legs. Its ankle joints, neck vertebrae, and long, flat skull were definitely crocodilian.

During the Jurassic, some members of the crocodile order took up a totally aquatic lifestyle. Ten-foot-long *Metriorhynchus* (MEE-tree-oh-RINK-us) sported clawed flippers and a strong, fishlike tail. It moved easily through the shallow seas that covered Europe and may have ventured out into deeper ocean as well. Remains of this creature have been found in Chile. That portion of the South American continent was submerged at the time and formed a shallow shelf that dropped off into the deeper waters of Panthalassa.

The modern crocodile, alligator, caiman, and gharial belong to the suborder Eusuchia. The prehistoric eusuchians were widespread in the swamps, rivers, and lakes of the Cretaceous Period. They had scaly armor, sharp teeth, and powerful jaws, and probably used hunting techniques similar to those of their descendants. They were certainly formidable predators of the age, but in terms of size, *Deinosuchus* may have been the granddaddy of them all. Its name means "terrible crocodile." Working only from a fossilized skull discovered in the remains of a Texas swamp, scientists calculate that this animal may have been more than 50 feet long.

Your child may ask: Why did crocodiles survive to modern times when dinosaurs did not?

Scientists aren't certain, but it may have had something to do with the crocodile's habitat. It often lived in swampy water. The water may have offered some protection from the disaster that overtook the dinosaurs.

Frogs, Toads, Newts, and Salamanders

At some point in time, along the shore of some shallow sea or swamp, the first amphibian struggled onto dry land. It was probably a very short foray, but it might be considered "one small step for amphibians and one giant step for all vertebrates that followed." The subclass that included those amphibian pioneers died out early in the Mesozoic. The amphibians that we encounter now—frogs, toads, newts, and salamanders—began to show up at about that time. Anurans, the order that includes frogs and toads, got its start in the Early Jurassic Period. The oldest known frog is *Vieraella* (vy-RAY-luh). It had the shortened backbone and long jumping legs of its modern relatives. Newts and salamanders, of the order Urodela, appeared at the end of the period. One would be hard-pressed to distinguish *Karaurus,* the oldest known salamander, from one of its modern relatives.

Your child may ask: Were amphibians the first land animals?

No. Invertebrates such as millipedes were the first ashore. The amphibians were the first backboned animals to live on land.

The Birds

From ravens and eagles to larks and robins, few creatures have been as honored in poetry and song as the bird has. But many millions of years before humans would develop poetry and prose, birds were already preparing their nests, preening their feathers, and filling the air with song.

Although it is not a direct ancestor to modern birds, *Archaeopteryx* is commonly called the first bird. In 1986, however, scientist Sankar Chatterjee discovered the remains of a tiny creature he called *Protoavis* (proh-toh-AYV-is), which translates into "first bird." This creature seems to have predated *Archaeopteryx* by about 75 million years. There are indications that it may indeed be the first true bird, but the remains are still being carefully studied.

The birds diversified and expanded their realm incredibly during the Cretaceous Period. Most modern avian groups were established during that time, including the ratites (flightless birds such as the modern ostrich), woodpeckers, parrots, swifts, owls, pigeons and doves, shorebirds, birds of prey, penguins, songbirds, and hosts of others. Some have become extinct, but most continue in one form or another.

There was, however, a subclass of birds that certainly existed only during the Cretaceous—the Odontornithes (oh-don-TOR-nih-thees), or "toothed birds." There were two orders in this group; both were shorebirds that had long beaks lined with tiny, sharp teeth. The order Hesperornithiformes (HES-pur-or-nih-thih-FORM-ees) was comprised of flightless, web-footed sea birds that dove beneath the water's surface to capture meals of fish or squid. Members of the Order Ichthyornithiformes (IK-thee-or-nih-thih-FORM-ees), or "fish birds," were small, strong fliers that wheeled in the sky above the inland seas of North America, not unlike modern gulls that circle effortlessly above modern shores.

Ask your child: What are some of the benefits that flight offers?
Flight is a way to avoid predators. Animals also use flight to locate food sources.

Mammals

If you look on a map of Africa, near the southeastern tip you will find the country of Lesotho, which is not much larger than the state of Maryland. In 1966, tiny fossil remains of a shrewlike creature were found in Lesotho. This little animal, christened *Megazostrodon* (mega-ZOS-troh-don), was identified as a mammal because of its teeth. It had four different kinds that grew in two sets. *Megazostrodon* was an early member of the subclass Prototheria (proh-toh-THEER-ee-uh), or "first mammals." The only living representatives of this group today are the monotremes, egg-laying mammals that still exist in Australia, Tasmania, and New Guinea. It's a good bet that the earliest mammals reproduced along the same order and, like modern monotremes, the females may have produced milk to feed their young. About five inches long, *Megazostrodon* and other prototherians were most likely nocturnal, protected from the night's chill by a coat of fur.

The subclass Theria included marsupials, or "pouched mammals," and placental mammals (those that gave birth to well-developed young). The latter belonged to the infraclass Eutheria. During the Mesozoic, eutherians were generally mouse-sized and lived on a diet comprised of eggs, insects, seeds, or fruit. Four-inch-long *Purgatorius* was probably a tree-dwelling insectivore. It weighed only about three-quarters of an ounce. This tiny Cretaceous critter is quite interesting because, although only a single molar has been found, it is enough to indicate that this animal may have been one of the earliest primates, a group that would eventually include monkeys, apes, and humans. If you follow the human family tree back to the Mesozoic Era, you will find a creature much like *Purgatorius,* a creature that, unlike the dinosaurs, would manage to cross the threshold into the Cenozoic Era.

With your child: Learn how to identify and classify groups of mammals. On a sheet of notebook paper, have your child write these three headings across the top of the paper: monotreme, marsupial, and placental. These are the three types of mammals living today. Ask your youngster to look up two animals that go under each heading (kangaroo and opossum would represent marsupials, for example) and write them down. Then, list the characteristics that make these creatures both similar to and different from one another.

4

The All-Stars

In the dinosaur Hall of Fame, four species take center stage: *Apatosaurus, Stegosaurus, Triceratops,* and *Tyrannosaurus rex.* Their images are everywhere, gazing at us from lunch boxes and notebook covers, prowling across T-shirts, and peering out of toyshop windows. One can only speculate about the secret of this group's particular appeal to youngsters. Perhaps it is their large size. With the exception of *Apatosaurus,* each was the largest species known in its family group. Or perhaps their charisma lies in their familiarity. This ancient quartet has been revered by many generations of children ever since fossils of each animal were discovered in the "Bone Wars" of the late 1800s and early 1900s. But whatever the reason, these dinosaurs have a very special status.

APATOSAURUS

Classification: Diplodocidae, Sauropoda, Sauropodomorpha, Saurischia

Range: United States (Colorado, Oklahoma, Utah, Wyoming)
Period: Jurassic

Apatosaurus (uh-PAT-oh-sawr-us) means "deceptive lizard." It was given that name because it seemed to closely resemble another known reptile, which at first posed a slight problem. That, however, was only the tip of the iceberg. Since it was first discovered in July of 1877, this dinosaur has caused more than its share of confusion. It has been given several names, two different heads, and a disparate assortment of bones in the neck, tail, legs, and feet.

As you were growing up, you probably came to know and love this animal as *Brontosaurus,* or "thunder lizard," a fitting title since the ground surely shuddered under each footstep of this mighty giant. It seems, though, that *Brontosaurus* is more accurately known as *Apatosaurus.* The problem goes back to when Arthur Lakes, a collector for paleontologist Othniel Charles (O. C.) Marsh, found the remains of a huge creature in Colorado. Because of its size, Marsh decided to name the creature *Titanosaurus.* That name had already been taken, so, noting a deceptive similarity between certain spinal bones of this newly discovered creature and those of *Mosasaurus,* he settled on the name *Apatosaurus.* Two years later an almost complete skeleton of another creature was found in Como Bluff, Wyoming. Marsh dubbed this animal *Brontosaurus* and later attempted a reconstruction. (His effort was flawed, though, because it contained limb and foot bones of *Camarasaurus,* a more delicately built sauropod.) Nearly a century later, in 1975, two American paleontologists reexamined the original remains and found that *Brontosaurus* and *Apatosaurus* were one and the same. Because *Apatosaurus* was the first name given to this animal, it is the name that is now accepted.

The mixup didn't end there. When Lakes uncovered *Apatosaurus,* its skull was nowhere to be found, but he did uncover a skull some four miles away. Marsh reconstructed *Apatosaurus* using that skull. In 1909 fossil hunter Earl Douglass found a set of remains but a disattached skull closely associated with that find was unlike Marsh's specimen. Scientists couldn't agree on which was correct, so the head was left off when the remains of *Apatosaurus* were displayed. Later, a cast of a *Camarasaurus* skull was added to the exhibit. It would remain there until 1979, when researchers reconsidered the evidence and the body of *Apatosaurus* was reunited with its proper head. It seems that Douglass had been right all along.

There has been no confusion over the size of this animal. From nose to tail, it was more than 70 feet long and stood more than 15 feet high at the hips. A fully grown adult weighed more than 30 tons, or about as much as a 95-cubic-foot block of solid lead. Early portrayals of *Apatosaurus* depicted it wading in shallow lakes or swamps, feeding on the soft aquatic plants that blanketed the murky water. Actually, this dinosaur lived on drier ground and ate ferns and the needles and twigs of pine, fir, and sequoia. The initial misconception grew out of the fact that the dinosaur was so large. People believed water helped buoy up its great body. On the contrary, *Apatosaurus* was well equipped to handle its own bulk. It had muscular, pillarlike legs, and broad, flat feet to bear the weight. *Apatosaurus* was engineered for size but not speed. Measurements made of fossilized tracks show that it seldom moved faster than five miles per hour. For humans that's a brisk trot.

Obviously, a quick exit was not an option when this dinosaur was confronted by a ravenous meat-eater. Nevertheless, *Apatosaurus* was not defenseless. On the inside toe of each front foot it harbored a curved claw. When threatened, this huge dinosaur might have reared up on its hind legs, balanced by its powerful 30-foot-long tail, to wield the claws as weapons. Also, *Apatosaurus*'s long tail might have been used to knock an enemy off balance. Still, its best protection was probably size. *Apatosaurus* could have trampled an attacker to death as modern elephants have been known to do to dispatch aggressive lions.

The Jurassic had its share of predators as fierce and as deadly as the lions of the Serengeti. *Allosaurus* was a formidable carnivore of that period, and deep gouges on some *Apatosaurus* remains demonstrate the proficiency of sharp *Allosaurus* teeth. Still, safety lies in numbers, and it appears that *Apatosaurus* traveled in large herds. The juveniles trekked along in the center of the herd where they would be more secure during an attack. Not a bad strategy, but predators probably followed the herd, waiting to pounce on any young or sick dinosaurs that lagged behind.

In many ways size can benefit an animal, but it also poses problems. *Apatosaurus*'s main priority was keeping itself fed. The huge sauropods had to consume upward of 500 pounds of food each day. Fortunately, the Jurassic was a period of lush, plentiful vegetation, and these animals clearly spent a great deal of time feeding. Surprisingly, the head of *Apatosaurus* was no larger than that of a modern horse, about 22 inches long, and its teeth weren't very spectacular either. They were peg-shaped, crowded toward the front of the animal's mouth, and not well suited for chewing up several hundred pounds of leaves every day. The key word here is *chew*, and it seems that *Apatosaurus* didn't. It lacked the muscles that could move the jaw from side to side as humans have. The current theory is that the animal did not chew but used its teeth to rake leaves and twigs into its mouth. It may have had a special chamber in its stomach, called a gizzard, which is specially designed for grinding and crushing food. Modern crocodiles and many birds have gizzards, so by watching them we can guess how a similar system might have worked for *Apatosaurus*. On occasion the animal swallowed several pebbles or stones that traveled only as far as the gizzard. Then, as food moved through, muscles in the walls of the gizzard churned and the stones (called gastroliths) rolled around, pounding and crushing the food into digestible pulp. But this is still speculation. Small piles of stones have been found in the stomach area of fossilized sauropods, but, although they are smooth and highly polished, there is no guarantee that they spent any time in the creature's belly. The evidence, as tantalizing as it is, remains circumstantial.

With your child: For the most part, the great sauropods died off at the end of the Jurassic Period. Some survived, and one in particular, *Saltasaurus,* developed protective plates on its back. Have your child draw a picture of how he or she thinks *Apatosaurus* would look if it had survived to modern times.

STEGOSAURUS

Classification: Stegosauridae, Stegosauria, Ornithischia
Range: Western North America
Period: Jurassic

Fossils of stegosaurids have been found in Europe, Africa, China, and India, but the most illustrious member of this family was *Stegosaurus* (steg-oh-SAWR-us), "plated" or "roofed lizard," a native of Jurassic North America. The first remains of *Stegosaurus* were discovered in 1876 in Colorado. Soon after, many more fossils (including those of a wolf-sized juvenile) were uncovered in Wyoming, Oklahoma, and Utah.

The most striking characteristic of *Stegosaurus* was the row of triangular plates that ran along its neck and back. The largest of these bony plates, those above the hips, were nearly three feet high and three feet wide. Stegosaur plates were not skeletal components but rather bony embellishments embedded in the skin. Paleontologists aren't certain how these plates were arranged on a living dinosaur. Until recently, the creature was shown with two distinct rows, but new evidence suggests that the plates may have been arranged in one alternating row along the spine.

What were the plates used for? Defense has been ruled out. Even though the plates may have guarded the spinal column, the animal's flanks and tender underbelly would have remained vulnerable. It's more likely that the plates were heat exchangers. This dinosaur could have turned the huge plates toward direct sunlight to warm the blood flowing near the surface, much the way solar panels heat water. To cool off,

Stegosaurus could turn the plates away from the sun. The optimal arrangement for the plates to be used in such a manner is a single row with the ends overlapping slightly.

> **Your child may ask:** How do we know that a single row is the best arrangement for *Stegosaurus*'s plates?
> Experiments conducted with similar plates in a wind tunnel showed that this arrangement is ideal for exchanging heat in a breeze.

In an age of giants, *Stegosaurus* did not stand out, but it was a fairly large dinosaur. It was 30 feet long from nose to tail, 11 feet tall at the hips, and it weighed between two and three tons. Like other Jurassic behemoths, *Stegosaurus* had strong, straight legs to support its tremendous weight, and its toes were tipped with heavy hooves. Its forelegs, though, were shorter than its massive hindlegs. This layout meant that *Stegosaurus* was probably a slow-moving dinosaur. Lacking speed, the plant-eater needed other methods to defend itself. Bony knobs clustered on its throat and studded over its hide probably gave it some protection from the slashing teeth and claws of the likes of *Allosaurus*, but *Stegosaurus*'s best weapons were at the end of its heavy tail. Two to four pairs of sharp spikes (depending on the species), each about three feet long, tipped this dinosaur's muscular extremity. If *Stegosaurus* was threatened, it could turn its back and lash its huge tail from side to side to knock an attacker off-balance or drive a deadly spike into the enemy's flanks.

Stegosaurus was not an aggressive beast. It was probably a solitary browser that wanted to be left alone. At the tip of its low, narrow 16-inch-long head was a small, bony beak designed to shear plants and leaves. Behind the beak, its jaws were lined with many small, leaf-shaped teeth. Since the teeth and jaws were rather weak, it's likely that *Stegosaurus* swallowed its food almost whole. Its meal may then have been ground up by gastroliths or perhaps allowed to ferment in the animal's huge vatlike stomach. Like *Apatosaurus*, *Stegosaurus* needed enormous quantities of food to keep its massive body supplied. Because of its configuration, it was simpler for the animal to graze on ground-level plants but, supported by its strong tail, *Stegosaurus* may have raised up on its hind legs to reach low tree branches.

When O. C. Marsh studied the fossilized skull of this extraordinary creature, he was surprised to find that the brain must have been no larger than a golf ball and weighed little more than two ounces. In comparison, the brain of a human weighs about three pounds. There is a puzzling area, however, near the creature's hips that was 20 times larger than the brain case. In the past, this has been called a "second brain," which is misleading. It was more likely a place where many nerves met, creating a sort of command center that helped the animal control its hind legs and tail, or perhaps it served as a fat-storage area. Still, even though *Stegosaurus* was not equipped with a second brain, the one it had must have filled its needs because these dinosaurs endured successfully for millions of years.

TRICERATOPS

Classification: Ceratopsidae, Ceratopsia, Ornithischia
Range: Western United States and Canada
Period: Cretaceous

"Horns as long as a hoe handle and eyes as big as your hat!" When John Bell Hatcher, a professional fossil collector, heard that statement he knew he was on to something important. In 1888, while searching for specimens in Wyoming, Hatcher met a cowboy who had chanced upon a considerable and most unusual fossil. Hatcher followed the lead and located the remains of a very large horned dinosaur. Unearthing a sample, he sent it immediately to O. C. Marsh for study. Hatcher followed up his initial find by uncovering the remains of more than 30 animals that represented several different species of the genus *Triceratops.* Marsh christened the first of these discoveries *Triceratops horridus* (try-SAYR-uh-tops HOR-ih-dus), which means "terrifying three-horned face." The name was an obvious choice. On its massive snout, this animal sported a thick, stubby horn, and above its eyes were two bony brow horns that grew up to four feet in length. (It wasn't the first time that Marsh had examined ceratopsian fossils. A year earlier he had misidentified the horncores of a smaller species of *Triceratops* as originating from an extinct variety of buffalo.)

Triceratops was almost as tall and as sturdily built as an elephant. It stood about 8 feet high at the shoulder, measured nearly 25 feet in length, and weighed in at between 6 and 8 tons. Even for a dinosaur of its great size, *Triceratops* had a monumentally large head. One well-preserved fossil skull measures 7 feet long and so accounted for nearly one-quarter of the total length of the living dinosaur. Its dimensions weren't the only exceptional aspect of *Triceratops*'s head. The back of the skull extended out to form a solid, bony frill tipped with a strand of bony knobs fixed along the edge. The frill may have added protection to *Triceratops*'s neck during an attack. It certainly added substance, for the animal's skull weighed more than a ton. The first three vertebrae behind *Triceratops*'s head were fused together to add strength and help the animal cope with its incredible burden.

Like all ornithischians, this dinosaur was an herbivore. Its long snout ended in a curved, horn-covered beak designed for clipping tough branches and for shearing off leaves and twigs. The animal could probably snap a two-inch-thick sapling with ease. The dinosaur also had a battery of strong cheek teeth which functioned like scissors to cut the vegetation into smaller, more digestible pieces.

Triceratops was extremely abundant at the end of the Cretaceous Period. Quite a few species of this animal have been recognized, based on slight differences in the size and shape of the skull. Research is still continuing, however, and it's possible that some of these animals represent not separate species but only variations within the same species due to sex, age, or individual dissimilarity. Great numbers of these ubiquitous ceratopsians may have traveled together in herds with juveniles safely in the center of the group. Perhaps meat-eaters stalked the herds, hoping for a young or weak dinosaur to stray within reach, but although *Triceratops* didn't look for trouble, it was certainly able to handle whatever came its way. A healthy, agile adult *Triceratops* wasn't a prime target for most carnivores, but a youngster could have been a temptation for a hungry *Tyrannosaurus.* If such an enemy posed a threat, the adults may have formed a defensive circle around the young. A herd of enraged *Triceratops* with their horns lowered would surely persuade even the most savage hunter to look elsewhere.

Your child may ask: Was defense the only purpose for *Triceratops*'s horns?

Probably not. Males may have locked horns with each other in combat over mates or territory, or to establish dominance within the herd. Fossil *Triceratops* horns sometimes show deep battle scars.

TYRANNOSAURUS REX

Classification: Tyrannosauridae, Carnosauria, Theropoda, Saurischia
Range: Western United States and Canada
Period: Cretaceous

The brightest in this gallery of prehistoric stars belongs to *Tyrannosaurus rex* (ty-ran-oh-SAWR-us REKS), the "king of the tyrant lizards." To date, however, this royal beast has been among the least understood of the dinosaurs. The other creatures in this chapter were plant-eaters, which were more numerous than their flesh-devouring counterparts. Until recently, only the partial remains of seven of these tyrannosaurids had been found. But in 1990, the king made two surprise appearances. Two nearly complete skeletons were discovered in Montana and South Dakota. It will be some time before the remains can be thoroughly studied, but many long-standing questions may soon be answered.

The first tyrannosaurid fossils—a few large teeth—were discovered in Montana in 1850, but the curious teeth were thought not to belong to a dinosaur. More than half a century later, fossil collector Barnum Brown uncovered the partial skeleton of a tremendous carnivore in Hell Creek, Montana. Three more years went by before Henry Fairfield Osborn finally described the remains of that beast in 1905 and chose the name *Tyrannosaurus.* In 1908 a skeleton with an excellent skull was found and the pieces of the puzzle fell into place. Scientists realized that the two fossil finds were from the same fearsome dinosaur, the largest flesh-eater that ever roamed the earth.

Tyrannosaurus rex towered nearly 20 feet tall. From nose to tail it was about 40 feet long, but individuals may have reached greater lengths. Weight estimates vary; some researchers believe this creature weighed a hefty eight tons, others believe it was a more svelte four tons. Either way, its three-foot-long jaws were packed with wickedly sharp teeth that were from three to seven inches long, serrated at the edges like steak knives, and curved slightly to give the animal a secure grip on its victims.

Your child may ask: Were all members of this family large?

A surprising answer to this question was found when a not-so-recent fossil discovery was recently "discovered." How is that possible? It seems that a dinosaur skull uncovered in 1942 has since rested at the Cleveland Museum under the name *Gorgosaurus.* Paleontologist Robert Bakker was not convinced. On closer study, he and his colleagues found that the skull was in fact that of a small tyrannosaur. In life the creature was only 16 feet long from nose to tail and about 600 pounds. What did they call this new mini-tyrannid? *Nanotyrannus,* of course—the pygmy tyrant!

There are different theories as to how *Tyrannosaurus rex* snagged its meals. According to one school of thought, *Tyrannosaurus* was a fairly slow, cumbersome animal that did not have the means to properly grasp active prey. It was viewed as a scavenger, relying on its keen sense of smell to locate carcasses of animals. *Tyrannosaurus* may have scavenged, but there is a mounting body of evidence that this dinosaur was perfectly capable of making its own kill. For one thing, *Tyrannosaurus rex* seems to have had stereoscopic vision. Able to focus both eyes forward at once on a single object, this predator could accurately judge a potential victim's distance. A large proportion of the brain appeared to be associated with the senses of sight and smell, a characteristic beneficial to an active hunter. In addition, *Tyrannosaurus*'s skull and flexible neck and head were heavily reinforced, probably to withstand the blows from a struggling animal, and it was equipped with powerful neck muscles that would have allowed it to snap and slash relentlessly at its prey.

It's possible that the tyrant king waited in ambush for a grazing hadrosaur to wander within range, then, mouth agape, it rushed at the unfortunate target. In spite of its great size, *Tyrannosaurus* showed certain adaptations for speed. It may have been able to close the gap between it and its prey with short bursts of speed up to 20 miles per hour.

There is another mystery waiting to be solved as well. For its size, this monstrous creature had ridiculously tiny arms no longer than those of an adult human. Though its fingers were tipped with sharp claws, *Tyrannosaurus*'s arms were too short to have been used as weapons or to grasp prey. The arms were even too short to reach its mouth, so they were useless for feeding. They may have been used, however, to push the carnivore up from a resting position. This animal had strong hips and a string of belly ribs (known as gastralia) that would have given it extra support when it was lying on the ground. When it wanted to stand again, it could have anchored its claws into the dirt, then pushed itself into an upright position.

Measurements made on the arm bones and muscle attachments of the recent Montana specimen indicate that the animal's small arms could have withstood a weight of 1,200 pounds. Whether that capability was directed toward a potential victim or simply to heft *Tyrannosaurus*'s own weight is, for the time being, unclear.

> ***With your child:*** Ask your child to stretch out belly down on the floor, then to get up slowly using her or his arms and hands. Have her or him try again without using arms. Was it more difficult the second time? Could this have been the way *Tyrannosaurus* used its arms? What are some other possibilities?

5

Other Dinosaurs
of Note

The all-stars extolled in chapter 4 are certainly the most celebrated dinosaurs, and one of them may be your child's favorite. Nevertheless, several hundred varieties of dinosaur roamed during Mesozoic times, and each had its own remarkable characteristics. Introducing your child to this assortment of creatures teaches him or her the concept of niches in the environment and shows them that an extraordinary spectrum of dinosaurs evolved to exploit those diverse habitats.

It's simple to carry this concept forward by taking your youngster on an excursion around the block or to a local park. Explain that modern animals take advantage of every possible habitat as you point out everything from birds nesting in trees to insects burrowing into the ground. Ask your child, "Which characteristics are most useful to each animal in its habitat? If the dinosaurs had not become extinct, what do you think they would look like and where would they live now?"

Wander through the following gallery of Mesozoic marvels as you will. You and your child may also enjoy "digging up" information and putting together a list of your own.

ALAMOSAURUS (AL-uh-mo-SAWR-us), "Alamo lizard"

Period: Cretaceous
Classification: Titanosauridae, Sauropoda, Sauropodomorpha, Saurischia

Length: 50 to 70 feet
Weight: 10 to 20 tons
Location: United States (Montana, Texas, New Mexico, Utah)

This giant represents one of the few sauropods to live during the Cretaceous Period. As the climate and terrain of the North American lowlands changed, sauropods were possibly supplanted by the duckbilled dinosaurs, and *Alamosaurus* was among the last of its kind. Named for the Ojo Alamo rock formation where it was first discovered, it could as easily have been named in honor of the Alamo in San Antonio, Texas, the site of another famous last stand. *Alamosaurus* was smaller than many earlier members of its infraorder, but still a leviathan of the period. Like its predecessors, the diplodocids, this dinosaur was slender (by sauropod standards), with a long neck and tail, a petite head, and weak, peglike teeth.

Your child may ask: Why did duckbilled dinosaurs replace the sauropods?

The huge sauropods had to eat hundreds of pounds of food every day. They must have spent most of their time just raking leaves and twigs into their tiny mouths. The duckbilled dinosaurs were better equipped when it came to feeding. They clipped leaves with their sharp-edged beaks, then ground up the food with their strong cheek teeth.

ALLOSAURUS (AL-oh-sawr-us), "different reptile"

Period: Jurassic
Classification: Allosauridae, Carnosauria, Theropoda, Saurischia
Length: 35 feet
Weight: 2 to 4 tons
Location: United States (Colorado, Utah, and Wyoming), Tanzania, Australia

Allosaurus may be gone, but it left plenty of traces behind. In one area of Utah alone, diggers uncovered the remains of 60 individuals. *Allosaurus* was named for the fact that its vertebrae were different from those of other dinosaurs. Large and solidly built, this meat-eater's strong jaws were abundantly endowed with curved two- to four-inch-long teeth, serrated along the edges for ripping and cutting. *Allosaurus* may have hunted and attacked its own prey, chased smaller predators away and fed on their kill, or may have simply been a scavenger.

> *Your child may ask:* What is a scavenger?
> A scavenger is an animal that feeds on waste material or the remains of a creature that is already dead. Many modern predators will not eat an animal they did not kill themselves. Others, such as the hyena, are able to capture a meal but will still feast on the meat that another predator has left behind. The vulture is one animal that feeds solely on "leftovers."

> *Ask your child:* Can you think of a way that scavengers help the environment?
> Scavengers clear away refuse left behind by other animals.

ANATOSAURUS (uh-NAT-oh-sawr-us), "duck lizard"

Period: Cretaceous
Classification: Hadrosauridae, Ornithopoda, Ornithischia
Length: 33 feet
Weight: 3 to 4 tons
Location: Alberta

Anatosaurus belonged to the highly successful duckbilled dinosaur group. Like others of its kind, it employed hundreds of cheek teeth arranged in several tightly packed rows. They formed a rough surface, sort of like a grater, which allowed the dinosaur to crush its food. Worn or lost teeth were constantly replaced. Not only do we know how it ate, but because of an incredible find, we suspect *what* it ate. Several mummified *Anatosauruses* have been discovered. Due to the dry conditions in the area where they perished, the skins and stomachs of the animals dried out instead of rotting away, and scientists have been able to identify the stomachs' fossilized contents—pine needles, cones, seeds, and fruit. Skin impressions showed signs of a speckled pattern, and stretchy skin between the toes is thought to be the remains of padding that cushioned the creature's feet as it walked.

> **With your child:** Collect pictures of different kinds of animals and ask your youngster to decide what sort of food the animal might eat based on the kind of teeth it has. Ask why humans have both slicing and grinding teeth.

ANKYLOSAURUS (an-KY-loh-sawr-us), "stiffened lizard"

Period: Cretaceous
Classification: Ankylosauridae, Ankylosauria, Ornithischia
Length: 25 feet
Weight: 3 to 4 tons
Location: North America (Alberta, Montana)

Largest and the last of the ankylosaurs, *Ankylosaurus* was well equipped for self-defense. Built low and wide, it was studded from head to tail with rows of bony plates, knobs, and spikes set into its leathery skin.

Even its eyes were protected by bony lids. This dinosaur was also equipped with rugged, curved claws on its feet. When attacked by a predator, it may have lowered its body and gripped the ground to protect its armorless underbelly. The creature's most effective weapon, however, was a huge double knob of bone at the end of its sturdy tail. If threatened, *Ankylosaurus* could swing this substantial club at an attacker. A well-placed blow could knock an enemy off its feet or even break its leg.

Your child may ask: What animals attacked *Ankylosaurus?*

This animal probably didn't have many enemies. Only a very large predator, such as *Tyrannosaurus,* may have tried to make a meal of *Ankylosaurus,* and even then, *Tyrannosaurus* would only pursue the animals that were very old, young, or sick.

AVIMIMUS (av-ih-MIME-us), "bird mimic"

Period: Cretaceous
Classification: Coelurosauria, Theropoda, Saurischia
Length: 3 to 5 feet
Weight: Undetermined
Location: Southern Mongolia

True to its name, this slim mini-dinosaur had birdlike feet and large eyes. Some scientists speculate that featherlike scales may have lined the trailing edges of this agile, vigorous animal's arms. If so, *Avimimus* might have used its forearms as broad, short wings to flutter along the ground, chasing insects to feed upon. There is also the possibility but no evidence that *Avimimus* may have had true feathers. If that proves to be accurate, the little hunter will move from the rank of dinosaur to the position of primitive bird.

Your child may ask: Are birds the only animals with feathers?

Yes. Feathers set birds apart from all other creatures in the animal kingdom. Feathers evolved from the scales, and both are made up of the same material—keratin—like your fingernails are.

Ask your child: What do feathers do for birds?

Feathers keep birds warm and enable them to fly. Colorful feathers can be used as camouflage or as a signal, such as breeding plumage.

BARYONYX (bar-ee-ON-iks), "strong claw"

Period: Cretaceous
Classification: Baryonychidae, Carnosauria, Theropoda, Saurischia
Length: 20 feet
Weight: 2 tons
Location: England

On a wintry day in January 1983, amateur fossil hunter Bill Walker explored a quarry near London. Something in the ancient clay drew his attention. It was the enormous, nearly 15-inch-long claw of *Baryonyx,* a most unusual carnivorous dinosaur. The low, crested, crocodilelike snout of this dinosaur housed 128 sharp, serrated teeth, twice the number found in most meat-eaters. Its long neck lacked the S-shaped curve typical of other large predators, and joined the head at an uncommon angle. Taking into account its powerful forelimbs, as well as fish scales found within the animal's body cavity, investigators concluded that this remarkable creature fished for its food. Crouching on the riverbanks or lake shores, *Baryonyx* waited patiently for its meal to swim close, then snagged the fish with the enormous, hooklike claw on its hand.

Your child may ask: What sort of fish did *Baryonyx* catch?

It may have fished for a creature like *Lepidotes* (leh-pih-DOHT-ees). This one-foot-long fish lived in seas worldwide and looked very much like a modern ray-finned American flagfish.

Ask your child: Can you think of a modern animal that catches fish similar to the way *Baryonyx* did?

Bears sometimes use their paws to scoop fish out of rivers and streams.

BRACHIOSAURUS (BRAK-ee-oh-SAWR-us), "arm lizard"

Period: Jurassic
Classification: Brachiosauridae, Sauropoda, Sauropodomorpha, Saurischia
Length: 75 to 85 feet
Weight: 80 to 90 tons
Location: Tanzania, Algeria, United States (Colorado)

We can only guess about certain aspects of a dinosaur's appearance. It would be short-sighted to discount the possibility of such accoutrements as flamboyant patterns or colorful dewlaps. In fact, the large size and unusual placement of *Brachiosaurus*'s nasal openings (on top of its head, centered above the eyes) suggest that it may have had a trunk—an interesting idea that is difficult to confirm. People once thought that the nostrils were positioned so that this long-necked dinosaur could wade into deep water for safety while keeping the top of its head above the surface, like a snorkel. Not so. To submerge its massive body completely, this giant would have needed at least 40 feet of water, and water pressure would have prevented the creature from drawing air down into its lungs. Protected by size, *Brachiosaurus* spent most of its time on dry land browsing in the treetops, much like a modern giraffe. Marks and wear on its chisel-like teeth show that it probably ate twigs and stems as well as leaves.

Your child may ask: How did this dinosaur get its name?

Brachiosaurus's odd name comes from the fact that its front limbs, or arms, were much longer than its hind limbs. The Greek word *brachio* means "arm."

Ask your child: Not everyone agrees that this dinosaur may have had some sort of trunk, but if it did, what do you suppose it would have been used for?

Brachiosaurus could have used its trunk for making loud calls or for gripping branches.

CHASMOSAURUS (KAZ-moh-SORE-us), "opening lizard"

Period: Cretaceous
Classification: Ceratopsidae, Ceratopsia, Ornithischia
Length: 17 feet
Weight: 3 tons
Location: Alberta

Chasmosaurus was one of the first long-frilled, horned dinosaurs. Fringed with spikes, its prodigious frill would have been too heavy for the animal to hold up if not for large skin-covered openings in the bone that lightened the frill (and earned the animal its name). Scientists believe that the frill anchored jaw muscles that gave *Chasmosaurus* its powerful bite. It was also used for display to discourage rivals and predators and perhaps to attract a mate. This ceratopsian had two long curved horns over its eyes and a shorter horn on its snout. The length of these horns may have depended on the sex of the animal, with the males sporting longer horns.

Your child may ask: Which dinosaur had the longest frill?

That was *Torosaurus* (TOR-oh-sawr-us), or "piercing lizard." The frill on this ceratopsian was 5½ feet long. Measured from the tip of its beak to the back of its frill, the skull was nearly 9 feet in length.

Ask your child: What animal living today has large facial horns?

A rhinoceros has one or two horns on its snout depending on the species.

COELOPHYSIS (SEEL-oh-FY-sis), "hollow form"

Period: Triassic
Classification: Podokesauridae, Coelurosauria, Theropoda, Saurischia
Length: 10 feet
Weight: 75 to 100 pounds
Location: United States (New Mexico, Massachusetts)

Millions of years ago, a herd of small, carnivorous dinosaurs trotted across what is now a part of the American West. Something, perhaps a flash flood, overwhelmed the band and others like it, causing their mutual demise. In 1947, while searching the red siltstones of Ghost Ranch, New Mexico, scientists uncovered the remains of about a hundred of the unfortunate creatures. As a result, *Coelophysis* is very well studied. It was a slightly built animal with a long, flexible neck and tail, and slender hind legs. Its clawed fingers were designed for grasping small prey, and jaws of its slim skull were lined with sharply pointed teeth. *Coelophysis* probably ate any creature it could catch, including insects, reptiles, and primitive mammals. After examining the material from Ghost Ranch, paleontologist Dr. Edwin Colbert concluded that *Coelophysis* even ate its own young.

Your child may ask: Why do researchers think that *Coelophysis* ate its own young?

The remains of babies were found within the stomach cavities of two or three of the *Coelophysis* at Ghost Ranch. These were not unborn animals but fully developed youngsters that seem to have fallen prey to hungry adults.

COMPSOGNATHUS (komp-soh-NAY-thus) "elegant jaw"

Period: Jurassic
Classification: Compsognathidae, Coelurosauria, Theropoda, Saurischia
Length: 2 feet
Weight: 8 to 10 pounds
Location: Germany, France

You may have heard that some dinosaurs were no larger than chickens. This diminutive dinosaur is the source of that comparison. It is identified from two sets of well-preserved fossils and named for the dainty character of its jaw and face. Although its tiny skull was only three inches long, this bipedal animal had an inventory of sharp little teeth and probably preyed on fast-moving insects and lizards that populated the islands of Jurassic Europe. *Compsognathus*'s birdlike appearance is strikingly similar to that of *Archaeopteryx,* but the little dinosaur also shared an unusual feature with giant *Tyrannosaurus:* both creatures had only two fingers on each hand.

Your child may ask: Was *Compsognathus* the smallest dinosaur ever found?

No. The smallest dinosaurs ever found were babies that would fit in the palm of your hand. *Compsognathus* is one of the smallest adults (see *Saltopus*).

DEINONYCHUS (dyn-ON-ik-us), "terrible claw"

Period: Cretaceous
Classification: Dromaeosauridae, Coelurosauria, Theropoda, Saurischia

Length: 10 to 12 feet
Weight: 150 pounds
Location: United States (Montana)

Deinonychus was fairly small and lightweight. Hardly a threat, you might think, compared to such a beast as *Tyrannosaurus.* On the contrary, what it lacked in size, this predator made up for in ferocity. Speed, agility, flexibility, excellent vision, sizable brain capacity, and a practice of hunting in packs made *Deinonychus* one of the most skilled and fearsome predators of the age. Its large jaw muscles and daggerlike teeth delivered a vicious bite, and its taloned, three-fingered hands were capable of tightly gripping prey. But its most dangerous weapon was found on its hind feet. The center toe of each foot was tipped with a savage claw. These five-inch-long talons were held up off the ground, safe from wear while the predator was running but could be quickly brought into action during an attack.

Your child may ask: How did this dinosaur use its huge claws?
    Deinonychus probably leapt at its victims, slashing them with the deadly hooks. It may have used its tail for balance during an assault. It may also have used the claw to tear open its kill.

DIPLODOCUS (dih-PLOHD-oh-kus), "double beam"

Period: Late Jurassic to Early Cretaceous
Classification: Diplodocidae, Sauropoda, Sauropodomorpha, Saurischia
Length: 85 to 100 feet
Weight: 10 to 12 tons
Location: United States (Colorado, Montana, Wyoming, Utah), Southern
England

For many years *Diplodocus* was thought to be the longest dinosaur. New findings have challenged this claim, but it is nonetheless an impressive beast. Like a living cantilevered bridge, the animal was supported by four ample, pillarlike legs, with its slender 30-foot-long neck stretched out in front, and its 45-foot-long whiplike tail trailing behind. The creature's broad, flat feet were similar to those of a modern elephant with five toes on each foot. Three toes on each hind foot and the inner toe of each front foot ended in thick curved claws. In small herds, *Diplodocus* marched through open forest and across wide floodplains, feeding on the cones and needles of conifers. It probably had few enemies and for the most part was able to browse in peace. Its lengthy tail, however, was capable of moving from side to side and could be used as a defense against an aggressor.

Your child may ask: Why is *Diplodocus* called "double beam"?
This dinosaur is named for special two-pronged bones in its tail that probably protected the tail from injury.

With your child: Discuss how a herd of these giant browsers might have changed a region as they moved through. If you can find such clippings or photos at a library, show your youngster pictures of the devastation left behind by a herd of migrating elephants and talk about the ways that the area can recover.

GALLIMIMUS (gal-ih-MY-mus), "rooster mimic"

Period: Cretaceous
Classification: Ornithomimidae, Coelurosauria, Theropoda, Saurischia
Length: 15 to 20 feet
Weight: 400 pounds
Location: Mongolia

Except for its tail and clawed arms, *Gallimimus* was built much like a modern ostrich. It was, in fact, the largest of the ornithomimids, or "bird mimics," also known as "ostrich dinosaurs," discovered to date. This dinosaur had a long, flexible neck, a horny, toothless beak, large eyes, and slender hind legs built for speed. According to some estimates, *Gallimimus* could sprint as fast as 35 miles per hour. Speed was a double bonus for this ornithomimid, for *Gallimimus* could outrun both predators and prey.

Your child may ask: How do scientists know how fast a dinosaur ran?

Stride is the distance between two footprints made by the same foot. The rate at which the animal was moving when it left the tracks can be determined by measuring that distance. The faster an animal runs, the farther apart the prints will be. The distance between prints also depends on the creature's size. In one stride, a very large *slow-moving* animal can cover the same distance as a *running* small animal.

HADROSAURUS (HAD-roh-sawr-us), "bulky lizard"

Period: Cretaceous
Classification: Hadrosauridae, Ornithopoda, Ornithischia
Length: 30 feet

Weight: 3 tons
Location: United States (New Jersey)

A typical duckbill, *Hadrosaurus* was a gentle plant-eater. There was little to set it apart from other hadrosaurs of the time. Although it was bipedal, this dinosaur ambled along just as easily on four feet. *Hadrosaurus,* however, has a modern claim to fame. Described in 1858 by Joseph Leidy, a professor of anatomy, it was the first dinosaur discovered and identified in North America. Leidy did not agree with the reconstructions that showed dinosaurs as plodding, four-footed animals. By studying a fairly complete skeleton from a New Jersey quarry, he deduced that this animal walked, at least at times, on its hind legs.

> ***Your child may ask:*** How do we know whether *Hadrosaurus* walked on two feet or four?
>
> By the structure of its legs and feet we can guess how an animal moved. *Hadrosaurus*'s forelimbs were considerably shorter than its hind limbs, and its hands were more delicate than its broad hind feet. These are traits of an animal that walked on its hind feet. The fact that it was equipped with hooflike nails on each of its limbs suggests that it spent time on all fours as well.

IGUANODON (ig-WAN-oh-don), "iguana tooth"

Period: Cretaceous
Classification: Iguanodontidae, Ornithopoda, Ornithischia

Length: 25 to 30 feet
Weight: 5 tons
Location: Europe, North America, Africa, Asia

Although it was the second to be described and named, *Iguanodon* was one of the first dinosaurs to be recognized as a previously unknown life form. During the Cretaceous, this dinosaur was extremely plentiful and widespread. Remains of this creature have been found on every continent with the exception of Antarctica. *Iguanodon* was able to walk on two legs or four and may have traveled in herds. The three middle fingers of each versatile, multipurpose hand ended in stubby hooves at the tips. The fifth finger could be used to grasp food, and its sharp, bony thumb spike could be wielded as a weapon. It took a while for scientists to correctly place the spikes. Since only one had been found among *Iguanodon*'s remains, the animal was restored with the curious appendage perched on its snout.

Your child may ask: How do we know *Iguanodon* traveled in herds?
In 1878, more than 30 adult dinosaurs were discovered together in a Belgian coal mine, which had once been a ravine. One explanation for finding so many creatures in one place is that they traveled in large herds, and whatever fate befell them claimed the whole group. Groups of fossilized trackways support the idea that *Iguanodon* moved in herds.

LAMBEOSAURUS (LAM-bee-oh-SAWR-us), "Lambe's lizard"

Period: Cretaceous
Classification: Hadrosauridae, Ornithopoda, Ornithischia
Length: 30 feet
Weight: 3 tons
Location: Alberta, Saskatchewan

Named in honor of vertebrate paleontologist Lawrence Lambe, *Lambeosaurus,* a duckbilled dinosaur, is to date the largest ornithischian ever found. True to its order, *Lambeosaurus* had a blunt, bony beak at the end of its snout and strolled slowly on four feet, but sprinted on two. Its most remarkable features were an odd, hatchet-shaped crest of hollow bone and a backward-pointing solid spike on its head. (All hollow-crested hadrosaurs are known as lambeosaurine.) There are several theories about the function of the crest. One proposal is that by passing air through hollow tubes within the crest, the animal may have produced loud bellowing or hooting calls. Perhaps it varied the sound to threaten a rival, advertise for a mate, or warn a herdmate of danger. Males probably had larger, more elaborate headgear than females.

> **With your child:** There is no way that anyone can say for certain whether dinosaurs snorted, whinnied, or roared, but it can be fun to guess. Together, look at pictures of different dinosaurs and try to imitate how you think they might have sounded.

MAIASAURA (my-ee-uh-SAWR-uh), "good mother lizard"

Period: Cretaceous
Classification: Hadrosauridae, Ornithopoda, Ornithischia
Length: 25 feet
Weight: 2 tons
Location: United States (Montana)

Maiasaura was a solid-crested hadrosaur. This dinosaur is fast becoming the most famous parent of all time. The discovery of a 75-million-year-old Maiasaur "nursery" in 1978 has revealed much about the family life of these animals, and in doing so has changed the way we view dinosaurs in general. The find included the remains of one adult, several three-foot-long babies, tiny 18-inch-long hatchlings, unbroken eggs, and empty eggshells. It seems that Maiasaurs were caring and attentive parents. In hollow mounds of dirt about seven feet wide, the female laid up to 15 eggs in several layers. Each layer was then covered with sand to keep it warm and hidden. The mother not only remained with her eggs until they hatched, but continued to feed and care for her brood until they were ready to leave the nest.

Your child may ask: How do we know that the parents took care of the babies?

The teeth of the babies in the nest showed wear from chewing up plant material that was probably gathered and brought to them by an adult.

With your child: Discuss how modern birds and other animals care for their young. A trip to the library or zoo will suggest questions such as: how are the young fed or do the parents protect the young?

MEGALOSAURUS (meg-uh-low-SAWR-us), "big lizard"

Period: Jurassic
Classification: Megalosauridae, Carnosauria, Theropoda, Saurischia
Length: 30 feet
Weight: 1 to 2 tons
Location: England, France

Although it's likely that *Megalosaurus* bones came to light in England as early as 1676, it wasn't until 1824 that this fierce beast became the first dinosaur to be named and described for the record. It was known only from a jawbone and teeth discovered by pioneer paleontologist William Buckland. *Megalosaurus* had a large head and flexible neck, a mouthful of saw-edged teeth, and dangerous claws on its fingers and toes. Unlike later flesh-eaters, this dinosaur's arms were strong and powerful, but it was only moderately built. Fossil footprints indicate that *Megalosaurus* walked with its toes pointed slightly inward. This may have made this great bipedal predator appear to waddle slightly when it walked.

> *Your child may ask:* How do we know how much a dinosaur weighed?
>
> One way to figure out the animal's weight is to make a model based on the creature's size and shape, then dunk the model in water. Animals generally are about the same density as water, so they displace their own weight. By measuring how much water is displaced by the model, scientists can calculate the weight of the actual animal.

MICROCERATOPS (my-kro-SAYR-uh-tops), "tiny horned face"

Period: Cretaceous
Classification: Protoceratopsidae, Ceratopsia, Ornithischia
Length: 2½ feet
Weight: Undetermined
Location: China, Mongolia

For dinosaur afficionados, an animal of small size can be just as intriguing as one of colossal dimensions. *Microceratops* was the compact model of the horned dinosaurs. A plant-eater, the little creature had a miniature frill and tough, parrotlike beak, but it lacked horns of any sort. *Microceratops* was lightly built and parted ways with most other ceratopsians in that, when hard-pressed, it could run on its two hind legs, although it likely spent most of its time on all four.

With your child: Within one animal family, there can be a wide range of sizes. Demonstrate this by putting together a picture collection of the largest and the smallest animals in certain groups—for example, horses, cats, and dogs.

OVIRAPTOR (oh-vih-RAP-tor), "egg stealer"

Period: Cretaceous
Classification: Oviraptoridae, Coelurosauria, Theropoda, Saurischia
Length: 6 feet
Weight: 100 pounds
Location: Mongolia

Oviraptor was related to ornithomimids ("bird mimic"). It was comparatively small, slightly built, and probably able to run at quite a clip. Its strong arms tapered down to clawed, grasping fingers tipped with sharply curved talons. Its skull, however, set it apart from others in its infraorder. A stubby hump, or crest, rose from *Oviraptor*'s beak, and its toothless snout was short, deep, and curved downward, capable of extraordinary crushing force. The animal's name is the result of convincing but circumstantial evidence. Its remains were first discovered just above the remains of a *Protoceratops*'s nest. Perhaps this "egg stealer" had been caught in the act of raiding the nest. *Oviraptor* probably also ate insects and fruit and scavenged whenever possible.

Ask your child: How do you suppose modern egg-laying animals protect their eggs from predators?
They hide them, bury them, or put them out of reach.

PACHYCEPHALOSAURUS (PAK-ee-SEF-uh-loh-SAWR-us), "thick-headed lizard"

Period: Cretaceous
Classification: Pachycephalosauridae, Ornithopoda, Ornithischia
Length: 15 feet

Weight: Undetermined
Location: United States (Wyoming, Montana)

Pachycephalosaurus, or "thick-headed lizard" was the largest of the bone-head dinosaurs. That is no reflection on its intelligence; the nickname refers to the creature's massive skull, which was 2 feet long and up to 10 inches thick . . . 20 times thicker than a human skull! Bony points and knobs ringed this unusual crown and also festooned the animal's short snout. It seems that this special headgear was not designed as a weapon but was used to battle other members of the dinosaur's own species in tests of strength. In 1955, Dr. Edwin Colbert suggested that *Pachycephalosaurus* behaved rather like modern sheep, with the males engaging in head-butting contests with one another. If that is true, a thick skull would definitely have been an advantage.

> ***Your child may ask:*** Did these dinosaurs get hurt when they fought?
> It's certainly possible that many pachycephalosaurs suffered from occasional headaches, but these creatures most likely didn't fight to the death. After a few collisions, the stronger of the two would claim his prize while his rival would slink away in defeat.

PARASAUROLOPHUS (PAR-uh-sor-ALL-oh-fus), "similar crested lizard"

Period: Cretaceous
Classification: Hadrosauridae, Ornithopoda, Ornithischia

Length: 30 feet
Weight: 3 to 5 tons
Location: Alberta, United States (New Mexico, Utah)

Parasaurolophus's slender snout supported a magnificent hollow crest that arched backward 4 to 6 feet. An interesting notch in the animal's backbone matched the furthest extent of the crest. When moving through dense growth, forest-dwelling *Parasaurolophus* may have fit the tip of the crest into the notch, creating a deflector that could easily brush aside small branches. Within the crest, paired nasal passages swept back from the nostrils, then curved forward again into the snout, an arrangement that probably enabled the animal to trumpet loudly as it moved through the trees. A plant-eater with a spoon-shaped beak, it dined on pine needles and the leaves of flowering trees such as oak and poplar. Researchers speculate this duckbill's noticeably deep, thick tail may have been brightly colored or patterned.

Your child may ask: What was this dinosaur's crest for?

It may have been multipurpose. The animal may have used it to produce sound, but air moving through the tube may have helped cool the brain as it circulated around the skull. This procedure may have improved the creature's sense of smell.

Ask your child: Your hands are multipurpose. How many different ways do you use them?

We use our hands for grasping food, manipulating tools, touching, dialing a telephone, playing a musical instrument, and so on.

PLATEOSAURUS (PLAY-tee-oh-SAWR-us), "flat lizard"

Period: Triassic
Classification: Plateosauridae, Prosauropoda, Sauropodomorpha, Saurischia
Length: 20 feet
Weight: Undetermined
Location: France, Germany, Switzerland

As one would expect of a creature that roamed the desert world early in the Mesozoic Era, *Plateosaurus* remains are found in Triassic sandstone and they are surprisingly plentiful. One of the earliest saurischians, this stocky animal could rear up onto its hind feet, but it most likely moved about on all fours. It had a small head, a long, sturdy neck, and a stout tail that made up at least half of the animal's length. *Plateosaurus* was a plant-eater with small, leaf-shaped teeth. Like other large herbivores it may have gathered in herds. Fortunately for *Plateosaurus,* carnosaurs such as *Megalosaurus* and the tyrannosaurids would not appear on the scene for several million years, even though the Triassic did have other predators. One little know beast, 20-foot-long *Teratosaurus* (teh-RAT-oh-sawr-us), or "monster lizard," clearly presented a danger. This animal was huge, lethal thecodont.

> ***Your child may ask:*** How do we know when these dinosaurs lived?
> The rocks that hold the fossil remains of these animals formed during the Triassic Period, so that is when *Plateosaurus* probably walked the earth.

PROTOCERATOPS (proh-toh-SER-uh-tops), "first horned face"

Period: Cretaceous
Classification: Protoceratopsidae, Ceratopsia, Ornithischia
Length: 6 to 9 feet
Weight: 400 pounds
Location: Mongolia

A stocky, sheep-sized creature, *Protoceratops* was an early horned dinosaur. Despite its name, it had no horns on its face (although some,
perhaps males, had a slighly bony rise above the beak). Still, it was one
of the first of the true ceratopsians and sported a sturdy, bony neck frill.
It was also the first of its suborder to walk full-time on all fours. An
herbivore, it cut the leaves and twigs of low-growing plants with its
parrotlike beak, then sliced the food using rows of shearing teeth. In
1923, an expedition to Flaming Cliffs in the Gobi Desert turned up a
Protoceratops nesting site. The little dinosaur had deposited its sausage-
shaped, eight-inch-long eggs in a large pit scooped out of the red sand,
but before they could hatch, the nest was buried by a sandstorm. This
discovery verified that dinosaurs were egg-laying animals.

>*Your child may ask:* Did all dinosaurs lay eggs?
>The answer to that question isn't settled. Some scientists specu-
>late that certain dinosaurs may have given birth to live young, but
>there is no proof. There is evidence, however, that dinosaurs did
>indeed lay eggs.

PSITTACOSAURUS (sih-TAK-oh-sawr-us), "parrot lizard"

Period: Cretaceous
Classification: Psittacosauridae, Ceratopsia, Ornithischia
Length: 8 feet
Weight: 50 pounds
Location: China, Mongolia

Psittacosaurus seemed to be a midway point between two different dinosaurs, ornithopods such as *Hypsilophodon* and ceratopsians such as *Protoceratops. Psittacosaurus* was not, however, a direct ancestor of the
horned dinosaurs that would develop later in the Cretaceous Period, but,
like them, it possessed a sharp, bony beak. Although this dinosaur did
not have horns or a definitive neck frill, it did bear a short, backward-
pointing spine at the edge of its skull. One variety had a hornlike lump on
its nose. *Psittacosaurus* often raised itself up from its short arms and
narrow, clawed hands to walk upright.

>*Ask your child:* Why do you think this dinosaur is named "parrot
>lizard?"
>*Psittacosaurus* was given its name because of its parrotlike beak.

SALTASAURUS (sahl-tuh-SAWR-us), "Salta lizard"

Period: Cretaceous
Classification: Titanosauridae, Sauropoda, Sauropodomorpha, Saurischia
Length: 39 feet
Weight: 6 to 10 tons
Location: Argentina

This is an animal that beat the odds. When other sauropods were dwindling, *Saltasaurus* prospered, but it had an edge over the others. Because it lived on what was, during the Cretaceous Period, the island continent of South America, it was cut off from many predators as well as the ornithopods that usurped the niches of its northern counterparts. That is not to say that there were no predators in South America. In fact, meat-eaters roamed the entire continent, which is a likely reason *Saltasaurus* developed a most interesting characteristic for a sauropod: it was armored. Its bony shield consisted of plates, studs, and tiny, horny spikes embedded in the hide of the animal's back and flanks.

Ask your child: Can you name some modern animals that use armor to defend themselves from predators?
    Armadillos, pangolins, and turtles all possess skin armor for protection.

SALTOPUS (SALT-oh-pus), "leaping foot"

Period: Triassic
Classification: Podokesauridae, Coelurosuria, Theropoda, Saurischia
Length: 2 feet
Weight: 2 pounds
Location: Scotland

Saltopus was one of the smallest and oldest known dinosaurs. Only about eight inches high, it was no bigger or heavier than a housecat. If a dinosaur could be termed "cute," this one might fit the bill, but its behavior was far from endearing. *Saltopus*'s slim jaws were lined with needle-sharp teeth that could deliver a serious snap. It fed on low-flying insects, speedy lizards, or any other small creature it could catch, and may have hunted in packs. At one time, people thought that this little dinosaur may have hopped or jumped from place to place, which accounts for its name, meaning "leaping foot."

> *Your child may ask:* Why would *Saltopus* have hunted in packs?
> *Saltopus* was so small that alone it could only capture tiny prey. Working together as a pack, these little predators could have brought down larger animals and shared the food. Today, this teamwork helps packs of modern wolves slay an animal as large as a moose.

SCUTELLOSAURUS (skoo-TEL-oh-SAWR-us), "little shield lizard"

Period: Jurassic
Classification: Fabrosauridae, Ornithopoda, Ornithischia
Length: 4 feet
Weight: 20 pounds
Location: United States (Arizona)

The earliest family of ornithopods was the Fabrosauridae (fab-roh-SAWR-ih-dee), named after a French entomologist. Covered by tiny, bony plates, *Scutellosaurus* is the only armored fabrosaurid known. (There is now some disagreement on this). It was first described by Dr. Edwin Colbert in 1981. Extremely lizardlike in appearance, this plant-eater gobbled up and swallowed mouthfuls of leaves without chewing them. Bipedal *Scutellosaurus* was equipped with claws rather than the hooves of the ornithopods that would develop later.

With your child: Armor is only one way plant-eaters defend themselves from predators. Make a list of other methods modern animals use. For example, modern elephants rely on size. The rhinoceros has large horns, and the hippopotamus has powerful jaws and sharp canine teeth. Once you have completed your list, imagine how these defenses might have worked for dinosaurs.

SPINOSAURUS (spy-noh-SAWR-us), "spiny lizard"

Period: Cretaceous
Classification: Spinosauridae, Carnosauria, Theropoda, Saurischia
Length: 40 feet
Weight: 7 tons
Location: Egypt, Niger

In many respects, *Spinosaurus* was like most other large meat-eaters. Solidly built, its hands and feet ended in sharp, curved claws, and its jaws were studded with needle-sharp teeth that were straight, not curved. The feature that set *Spinosaurus* apart was the peculiar sail on its back. The sail was composed of leathery skin stretched across a fan of supporting spines, the tallest of which stood more than six feet high. The sail may have been used as a heat exchanger to warm or cool the animal. As the morning sun rose in the sky, this fierce carnivorous dinosaur probably lounged with its sail exposed to the warming sun. Rapid warming gave this predator an overwhelming advantage over prey that may have been sluggish from the cool night before.

Ask your child: How might this dinosaur have used its sail to cool off?

Since the sail may have been a heat exchanger, *Spinosaurus* might have simply turned it away from the sun to cool itself.

STAURIKOSAURUS (stor-ik-oh-SAWR-us), "cross lizard"

Period: Triassic
Classification: Staurikosauridae, Dinosauria?
Length: 6 feet
Weight: 30 pounds
Location: Brazil

Dr. Edwin Colbert first introduced this dinosaur to the world in 1970. Although it is only known from a few remains—the lower jaw, most of the vertebrae, the pelvis, and parts of the hind legs—these are enough to deduce that the animal was a very primitive theropod (a bipedal meat-eater). In fact, *Staurikosaurus* may mark the early beginning of the theropod record. It had a long, toothy jaw, a slender body, and the legs of a bipedal, running animal. It was found in southern Brazil, where the constellation known as the "southern cross" dominates the night sky.

Your child may ask: If only a few bones are found, how do scientists know what the animal really looked like?

They don't know for certain, but by comparing the creature to similar animals that lived at the time, as well as to modern animals, scientists can make an "educated guess" about the appearance of a dinosaur. Some dinosaurs have been described from as little as a fossil tooth.

STENONYCHOSAURUS (sten-ON-ik-oh-SAWR-us), "narrow-claw lizard"

Period: Cretaceous
Classification: Saurornithoididae, Coelurosauria, Theropoda, Saurischia
Length: 6-1/2 feet
Weight: 30 to 50 pounds
Location: Alberta, United States (Montana)

Mystery surrounds this animal. It may be the same as two other Cretaceous coelurosaurs, *Troödon* (TROH-oh-don) meaning "woundtooth," and *Saurornthoides* (sore-or-nih-THOYD-eez), meaning "birdlike lizard." The question is yet to be resolved, but there are a few things that we are certain about. *Stenonychosaurus* had a large brain for its size and was quite intelligent for a dinosaur. The areas of the brain devoted to the animal's senses and reflexes were well developed, adding to the concept of this predator as nimble and capable. Speed and keen vision would have been useful for both avoiding enemies and catching prey. This dinosaur (also known as the Cretaceous coyote) may have hunted small mammals that only came out of hiding in the dim light of dusk, and it is a good candidate for acceptance as a warm-blooded dinosaur.

> *Ask your child:* Why would the ability to hunt in the dark have been an advantage for this animal?
> It would have had less competition when hunting. Other predators that might have preyed upon it or on what it ate would not have been active.

STYRACOSAURUS (sty-RAK-oh-SAWR-us), "spiked lizard"

Period: Cretaceous
Classification: Ceratopsidae, Ceratopsia, Ornithischia
Length: 17 feet
Weight: 4 tons
Location: Alberta, United States (Montana)

In life, this six-foot-tall animal must have been a frightening-looking beast. It was a short-frilled ceratopsian with a startling, bony collar. Many small points lined the sides of the frill, and six tremendous spikes protruded along the back arch. *Styracosaurus* had a single but impressive 2½-foot-long nose horn above its downturned beak. As with other short-frilled ceratopsids (with the exception of *Triceratops*) there were openings in the frill to make it lighter. Even so, this animal had to be very powerfully built around the shoulders to wield its massive head.

> ***Your child may ask:*** Did this dinosaur use its frill horns as weapons?
> Probably not. Because the horns stuck out from the frill, their purpose was likely to make the animal look even larger and more ferocious.

SUPERSAURUS (SOO-per-sawr-us), "super lizard"

Period: Jurassic
Classification: Sauropoda, Sauropodomorpha, Saurischia
Length: 100 feet
Weight: 50 tons
Location: United States (Colorado)

This titan is known from a few remarkable bits and pieces; an eight-foot-long shoulder blade, a six-foot-wide pelvis, several ten-foot-long ribs, and neck vertebrae that reach five feet in length. Discovered by James Jensen of Brigham Young University, the estimated body length of *Supersaurus* is nearly 100 feet, and its height could top 50 feet. But it still may not be the largest of the sauropods. In 1979, Jensen discovered a shoulder blade in Colorado that measured nearly ten feet. The original owner of this bone may have been 100 feet long, 60 feet tall, and may have weighed 80 tons. For the time being it is known as *Ultrasaurus.* But in this contest of size, we may not yet know all of the contestants. In New Mexico in 1985, Dr. David Gillette unearthed fossil remains of a behemoth he has dubbed *Seismosaurus,* a creature that may have stretched more than 120 feet in length and weighed nearly 100 tons!

> *Your child may ask:* It is possible that a dinosaur even larger than *Seismosaurus* existed?
>
> It's possible, but at a certain point, great size becomes a disadvantage. Imagine how much food the giant sauropods had to eat!

WUERHOSAURUS (woo-er-hoh-SAWR-us), "Wuerho lizard"

Period: Cretaceous
Classification: Stegosauridae, Stegosauria, Ornithischia
Length: 20 feet
Weight: 2 to 3 tons
Location: China

Paleontology is a dynamic science. A single discovery—a tooth, a claw, the impressions of a feather—can force theories to be modified, modernized, or simply replaced. This dinosaur was the first stegosaur found to have lived during the Cretaceous Period. The belief that stegosaurs had absolutely become extinct by the close of the Jurassic was shattered by a few fragments of bone. From the paltry evidence, *Wuerhosaurus* appears to have been a typical stegosaur. Its plates, however, may have been flattened at the edges rather than narrowed to a point, as Stegosaurus' were.

With your child: *Wuerhosaurus* is an excellent example of the changing face of paleontology. If you are able to find very old books or posters about dinosaurs at your library, look through them with your child to find other theories that have been altered over the years. Point out to your youngster that this branch of science, like all others, is part of an ever-evolving process, and that one of the most useful tools a scientist can have is an open mind.

6

The Demise of the Dinosaurs

Everyone loves a good mystery, and the disappearance of the dinosaurs has all of the elements needed to challenge even the greatest of sleuths. First, there is no shortage of victims. Fifty to sixty-five percent of species living on Earth at the end of the Cretaceous Period seem to have disappeared from the fossil record at about the same time. In addition to the the dinosaurs, the list of casualties includes pterosaurs, sea organisms such as ammonites and forams, and large swimming reptiles such as mosasaurs and plesiosaurs. (A notable exception is the Crocodilia.) The scene of the crime is worldwide and the time of death is generally centered on the Cretaceous/Tertiary boundary, or K-T boundary.* What's missing from this prehistoric puzzle is the weapon of destruction. Still, there are many clues, so why not challenge your youngster to examine the evidence and come up with a possible solution. Remind your child that, like a good detective, a good scientist asks lots of questions and never takes anything for granted.

SENSE AND NONSENSE

There are dozens of proposals about how the dinosaurs ultimately met their end. A few ideas are silly, such as "the dinosaurs were hunted down

---

*You may wonder why the Cretaceous/Tertiary boundary is represented by the letters K-T. The T is easy—it's for Tertiary. The K needs a bit of explaining. The Cretaceous period was named for layers of chalk formed during the time. The Greek word for chalk is *creta*, also spelled *kreta*. Why not just call it the C-T boundary? Because it might be mistaken for the earlier Carboniferous Period.

by little green men in flying saucers." (You may have also seen artist Gary Larson's "The Far Side" cartoon suggesting that the dinosaurs smoked too much.) Most serious theories, however, are based on at least some evidence. Examining these proposals with a critical eye is a fine way to demonstrate to your child the difference between theory, fact, and fancy. Point out that a fact is something that we are relatively certain of. For example, based on fossil evidence, which includes bones and footprints that can be physically measured, we are reasonably certain that *Tyrannosaurus rex* was a large dinosaur. To a lesser degree, by examining this creature's teeth and observing modern animals with smaller but similarly shaped teeth, we can offer a strong case for *T-rex* having been a meat-eater. Still, no one has ever observed this animal devouring a meal, so this theory is based on available information. Finally, although the "little green men from outer space" idea cannot be positively disproved, there is absolutely no evidence to support such a case and there are a great many reasons to reject the notion as pure fancy.

With this in mind, let's examine a few explanations for the extinction of the dinosaurs. In your own words, present each to your child and help her or him to discover a clue or clues that place each theory in doubt.

Death by Diet

A few scientists have suggested that a change in their menu may have sealed the dinosaurs' fate. If you look around today, most of the plants you see are angiosperms (flowering plants). Throughout most of the Mesozoic Era, that was not the case. There were no colorful, fragrant blossoms, no flowing grasslands, no sweet, succulent fruit ripening in the warm sun. The plant-eating dinosaurs fed only on lush copses, thickets, and forests of ferns, conifers, and cycads. It was not until the early- to mid-Cretaceous, at least 40 million years before the end of the period, that the first flowering plants appeared. As new forms developed and spread, dinosaurs were presented not only with cones, leaves, and twigs, but a cornucopia of fruit and seeds to eat.

Were these new foods too tough to eat or even poisonous?

This is not likely. One clue is that, although the plants were new-comers to the Mesozoic Era, they had developed about 40 million years before the dinosaurs died out. That should have been plenty of time for the animals to get used to a new diet! Also, this idea does not explain why so many sea creatures died off as well.

Death by Distress

Difficulty in finding food and shelter may have made dinosaurs nervous and stressed. As a result, they began to lay weak, thin-shelled eggs that could not survive long enough to hatch. In addition, certain dinosaurs and small mammals may have preyed upon unprotected eggs, so fewer dinosaur babies were born.

Did weak dinosaur eggs and egg-devouring mammals bring about a worldwide catastrophe at the end of the Cretaceous Period?

The clue here is *worldwide.* This theory does not explain what caused the extinction of sea creatures, particularly the ichthyosaurs, which didn't even lay eggs. Although egg-eating animals or thin shells may have added to the dinosaur's problems, it is unlikely that these challenges alone could have wiped them out completely.

Eradication by Radiation

One popular theory suggests that a tremendous, powerful explosion of a not-too-distant star formed a supernova that bathed Earth in deadly cosmic radiation. This inescapable, lethal event could have doomed animals on both land and sea.

Were the dinosaurs and many of their sea-going neighbors the victims of a stellar blast?

Once again, the clue is in the pattern of extinction. This theory explains why many animals died, but it does not explain why so many survived. It isn't likely that crocodiles, turtles, birds, and mammals would have lived through such an ordeal. In addition, astronomers have not located traces of any such celestial explosion that would fit this scenario.

Tertiary Teeth

Some paleontologists question that the dinosaurs actually became extinct 65 MYA. One scientist points to fossils found within Tertiary rock of the early Cenozoic Era. The rock that holds these fossils (mostly dinosaur teeth) formed well after the Cretaceous Period had faded away.

Did the dinosaurs actually survive beyond the K-T boundary?

This possibility shouldn't be ruled out, but the present evidence is not strong. The clue here is that mostly *individual* teeth have been discovered. The fossil teeth may have eroded from Cretaceous rock by a river or stream, then were redeposited and sealed into sedimentary rocks that formed during the Tertiary Period. Until a whole or even partial skeleton is found in such rock, the K-T boundary is still the best bet as the finale for the age of dinosaurs.

CONTENDERS FOR THE TITLE

Okay, so none of the current theories are perfect, but two seem to stand out. Let's take a closer look at this popular pair.

Doom from Deep Space

One view that has gained tremendous favor is that the death blow was struck from space, not by little green men or exploding stars, but by an asteroid. The inspiration for this idea snakes through the ancient cliffs of Gubbio, Italy. In 1978, geologist Walter Alvarez visited the town. While studying ancient limestone rocks, a thin layer of clay caught his attention. From where it occurred in the rock, Alvarez could tell that it had been deposited near the end of the dinosaur age and around the dawn of the age of mammals. Later experiments performed by his father, Luis Alvarez, and colleagues at the University of California at Berkeley showed that the clay contained an element called iridium in quantities 30 times higher than in the layers above and below the clay. Iridium is very rare in the earth's crust but plentiful in meteorites and asteroids. Soot levels in the layer, possible evidence of firestorms, also proved to be many times higher than normal.

Of the thousands of asteroids whirling in orbit around the sun, at least 80 and probably many more cross the earth's orbit regularly. Recently, one passed only two moon orbits distant from our planet—an astronomical close call. You can reassure your youngster that the odds are less than one in 200 million that a very large asteroid will hit Earth anytime soon. Collisions have occurred in the past, however, and some paleontologists speculate that a devastating jolt took place right around 65 MYA.

Your child may ask: If an asteroid collision really happened, how would it affect life all over the planet?

Imagine this. Looming larger and larger in the heavens, a rocky object about as wide as Manhattan Island screams through Earth's atmosphere at up to 70 times the speed of sound. It smashes into the ocean, spewing up about 1,000 times the amount of seabottom rock and dust that was removed when the Panama Canal was dug. The ground trembles in an earthquake with 100,000 times more energy than the great San Francisco quake of 1906. Within seconds, a wave three miles high, the first of many, rushes over nearby shores, scraping them down to bare rock and flooding the land for hundreds of miles inland. In the earth's crust near the impact, minerals such as quartz shatter, and other minerals typical of cosmic crash sites, such as sanidine and stishovite, are forged.

Ground zero at the center of the impact is hotter than the surface of the sun. Seawater foams to 100,000 degrees F. The fiery blast heats the local atmosphere to more than 3,000 degrees F, and forests burst into flames fanned by hurricane force winds. Any living thing within 1,200 miles, land or sea, is instantly annihilated. The resulting firestorms send choking ash and smoke into the atmosphere, which is already blackened by thousands of tons of dust.

Within a few hours, Earth is encircled by a veil of this dust, which is 17 miles thick and cuts off warmth and light from the sun. Slowly the fierce heat dies away, and rain as caustic as battery acid begins to fall, followed by grimy snow as worldwide temperatures plummet to subfreezing. During the three to six months it takes for the skies to clear, green plants on land and phytoplankton in the sea are without sunlight and cannot manufacture food. Farther up the food chain, large plant-eaters soon starve and, deprived of prey, the meat-eaters follow.

This scenario is certainly the sort of thing that disaster films are made of, but is it fiction or fact? The crater from such a crash could be several miles deep and the size of Lake Michigan. Wouldn't this convincing evidence be easy to find? Not really. If the object fell on land, the crater, worn by centuries of wind and rain, would be hard to recognize. The odds are about three to one that such an impact would take place in the ocean, making the depression even more difficult to spot. A megacollision of this sort, however, would leave behind a telltale set of "prints." Recent research points to two possible locations for the smoking gun. Both are in the Caribbean, one near Cuba and the other off the northern coast of Colombia.

An Alternative Theory

A number of scientists agree with this theory on principle, but claim that the evidence came from Earth itself, not space. The iridium-laden clay layer could also point to an earthly culprit. Although there is little iridium on the earth's crust, there's much more in the molten rock beneath the crust. Perhaps the iridium, along with tons of dust, rock, and soot gushed to the surface by way of an erupting volcano.

One of the greatest volcanic blasts in modern history occurred in 1883 on an Indonesian island when infamous Krakatoa blew itself apart. The explosion was heard in the Indian Ocean over 3,000 miles away. Ash and dust in the area blocked out light from the sun for days. Traveling back through the geological record, it seems that 75,000 years ago a huge volcano tumultuously launched 400 times more fiery lava, rock, and ash into the air than Krakatoa did. One such blast may not completely change Earth's climate, but there may have been more than one explosion. About 66 million years ago in India, volcanic activity was greatly stepped up. For a period of about 300,000 years the volcanoes spewed and belched gas into the atmosphere in a series of tremendous eruptions.

Was the messenger of destruction an asteroid or a volcano? You may not have to choose. It isn't difficult to imagine that a cosmic collision could trigger worldwide volcanic action.

Other Extinction Explanations

A number of paleontologists, including Dr. Robert Bakker of the University of Colorado, suggest that the dinosaurs did not go out with bang but rather with a groan.

Although it feels solid enough, the ground beneath our feet is actually moving. Over millions of years the continents have crept across the face of the planet like slow-motion bumper cars. As the earth's dry land redistributes itself, sea levels rise and fall, often creating tremendous barriers and so segregating animal groups into pockets.

As the Cretaceous Period drew to a close, the continents were largely separated by miles of shallow seas and nascent oceans. At times, many animal groups developed in comparative isolation, and often adjusted to local bacteria and disease-causing agents. In some cases these animals may even have become carriers of disease. Even though they may not have experienced any immediate ill effects, the creatures presented a biological time bomb.

At the end of the Cretaceous, a great many land bridges pushed above the waves, and animals that had been separated for millennia were on the move, carrying their germs with them. Species mingled and became exposed to diseases for which they had developed no immunity. A deadly illness could have spread through an unprotected species like wildfire.

Sickness wasn't the only danger. Migrating predators may have wiped out animals that had never been exposed to their style of hunting and thus had not developed a means of defense. Herbivorous species migrating into a new area may not have been attractive to local predators. With nothing to keep them in check, these plant-eaters could overrun their new neighborhoods, supplanting existing species or quickly eliminating food resources. There are plenty of modern examples of such incidents. Just ask Australian farmers about the rabbits that have overpopulated their land.

The shifting positions of the continents brought about variations in the weather as well, making it more seasonal. As the climate cooled, lush, tropical forests were replaced by open forests. While land creatures fought to cope with their changing environment, changing sea levels could have wreaked havoc on sea creatures dependent on stable currents, salinity, and temperatures. This theory is also a good explanation for the extinctions at the end of the Jurassic Period, which appear to have claimed mainly large animals likely to migrate great distances as well as a wide variety of sea creatures.

Bakker does not disagree with the idea that there may have been some sort of collision with an extraterrestrial object at the K-T, only that it was not as cataclysmic as suggested and may not have been responsible for mass extinctions. He contends that frogs and turtles, among others, would have been unlikely to survive the severe cold and acid rain in the aftermath of a major asteroid collision. However, these small, sedentary, swamp or lake-dwelling animals would probably not have joined a great continental exchange, and so, unlike the dinosaurs, could have made a healthy transition to the Cenozoic Era.

It's likely that the final answer is a combination of the theories discussed here. The fossil record seems to show that the number of dinosaur species was already decreasing long before the fateful K-T boundary. Those common in the fossil record in Alberta and Montana went from 30 main groups (general) 73 MYA to some 13 groups about 66 MYA.* No matter what its nature, each blow may have just put another nail in the inevitable coffin. When asked for his opinion on what killed the dinosaurs, paleontologist Jack Horner says he really doesn't care. "The dinosaurs were a fascinating and remarkable group of animals that survived for millions of years, and that is far more interesting than what killed them."

>***With your child:*** As you can see, theories are only as good as the information that can be obtained to support them. One way to make this clear to your youngster is to find a local "case" to solve. If you look around your neighborhood or local park, you may come across the remains of a tree that is dead or failing. The project will be to discover what has damaged the tree. (If your "test subject" is on private property, be sure to ask for permission from the owner first.) Have your child make up file cards with headings such as "Weather," "Insects," and "Soil" to help organize notetaking. Next, guide him or her in studying the tree and its surroundings. Go to the library and find out what variety it is, where it grows best, and what a healthy specimen looks like. Discover which insects may prey upon the tree and find out if such creatures are common in your area. Study other plants nearby to see if they, too, have been affected. You can get expert advice by taking samples of damaged leaves and bark to a neighborhood nursery or botanical garden. Encourage your child to theorize about what caused the problem and to support his or her conclusions with evidence. The goal here is to experience and to understand the process of discovery.

THE SURVIVORS

To round out your child's perception of the dinosaurs' fate, you may want to visit the zoo, an aquarium, or the seashore to observe modern descendants of the survivors. Turtles, snakes, lizards, insects, sharks and other fishes, crocodiles, primitive birds, and mammals are all survivors. The event or series of events that killed the dinosaurs eliminated about two-thirds of the plant and animal species on Earth. Why did one-third survive? Is there a common thread that pulled those animals through?

---

*This could have as much to do with inaccuracy of the fossil record as it does with the number of animals living at the time.

Ask your youngster to consider what traits might have made those creatures better able to deal with the problems that finally brought an end to the age of dinosaurs. Here are a few suggestions:

Not all the animals that endured won their continued existence on the same basis, but on land, small size seems to have been a plus. Many surviving species were made up of individuals generally weighing no more than 50 pounds. If the demise were a rapid one (caused by an asteroid impact, for example), smaller creatures would be better equipped to handle diminished food supplies. Tiny land-dwellers may have hidden in burrows to escape extreme temperatures. Modern snakes and other animals unable to outrun forest fires often seek shelter below ground, insulated from the heat and flame raging above. As temperatures dropped, warm-blooded, fur-bearing mammals or feathered birds would have had better protection against the cold while they scavenged for seeds or roots. Other creatures may have just "waited out" the bad times in some form of resting state, similar to what modern bears, ground squirrels, toads, insects, or lungfish do.

The two-foot-long, three-pound tuatara of New Zealand presents another theory. At the beginning of the Mesozoic Era, the tuatara's ancestors, the rhynchosaurs, (RINK-oh-sawrz) were fairly common. The modern female tuatara buries her eggs in deep burrows and leaves them. The eggs take up to 15 months to hatch, and the young can easily take care of themselves. If the ancestors of the tuatara did the same, disaster may have claimed the adults while the eggs made it safely through. The hatchlings would have been born into a very different world than that of their parents.

If the demise was triggered by a slow but steadily shifting climate, changing food resources or disease spread by the intermixing of foreign species, then less specialized animals and animals that tended not to migrate for appreciable distances (turtles, frogs, snakes, and perhaps crocodiles) could have been at lesser risk.

MORE SENSE AND NONSENSE

Touching on the difference between fact and fancy, you may want to mention to your child that some people claim to have sighted living dinosaurs or prehistoric reptiles still lurking in remote corners of the earth. The most famous of these, the legendary Loch Ness monster, denizen of the dark waters of Scotland's Lake Ness, is so well known that it even has a nickname, Nessie. The 900-foot-deep Lake Ness lies along a fault in the earth's crust. Millions of years ago, the fault slipped and cut off an arm of the sea, and some people believe this trapped one or several plesiosaurs. To defend their claims, Nessie-boosters provide blurry photographs of a dark object appearing at the surface of the water. But despite exhaustive searches, there is no hard evidence that such a creature inhabits the lake. As much as we would like to see a living dinosaur, that opportunity is not likely to present itself.

7

On the Fossil Trail

The word *fossil* conjures up images of skeletal tyrannosaurs stalking fleshless duckbills. That representation is accurate, but you might be surprised to discover that in one form or another fossils are all around us. Coal and oil are fossil fuels formed from ancient plants and microscopic animals. Tiny insects embedded in beads of fossilized tree resin, or amber, have long been prized as jewelry. Chalk is made up of the remains of microscopic sea creatures. Even the stone blocks used in buildings on Main Street (if they are cut from sedimentary rock) may house tiny fossils. Perhaps the best definition of *fossils* is that they are our key to Earth's past. Like detectives, paleontologists solve the mysteries of the dinosaurs by searching for clues, and fossils are one of the best sources of information.

Fossil is from the Latin *fossor,* or "digger." Sixteenth-century German scientist Agricola (Georgius) applied it to anything that was dug up from the earth—and that covered a wide range of objects and organisms. Actually, the fairly complete dinosaur skeletons we admire in museum displays are rare indeed. Probably fewer than one-tenth of one percent of all vertebrate remains even survived to become fossils. After death, many living things are eaten or eventually rot away, quickly disposed of by bacteria and fungi. Bones, teeth, and shells may be dissolved by chemical action. Without such processes Earth would be covered in refuse. On occasion, however, under ideal conditions, a fragment or an impression of a once-living organism may be preserved like a providential, though inexact, time capsule. It is via these scraps and tidbits that scientists have pieced together the story of the Mesozoic Era.

With your child: You and your youngster might enjoy putting together a time capsule of your own. A coffee can will make a nice capsule. Ask your child to think of small objects that would best represent him or her to someone opening the capsule 20 years from now. The objects should reflect his or her interests at the time as well as current events in your child's school or neighborhood, or even the world at large. A small toy (such as an action figure), a photograph, a magazine or newspaper clipping, an iron-on patch, a souvenir—any nonperishable item that fits easily into the can is acceptable. You may want to add an item or two of your own. When the capsule is filled, line the rim of the can with household cement and put the lid on. With a marker, inscribe the date on the lid. Place the can in a safe spot, perhaps on a high closet shelf, in the attic, or in a basement cupboard. Whether you or your child happen upon the capsule and decide to open it six months later or years later, the contents will certainly give some insight into your child's past.

How Do Fossils Form?

The variety of fossil known as a cast is formed when, for example, a shell drifts to the bottom of a pond and is covered by fine mud, which hardens into rock, sealing the shell inside. Over millions of years the object disintegrates within its stony tomb, leaving behind an empty space called a mold. Over the course of additional millennia, minerals seep in to fill the cavity. The assortment of minerals that have been discovered in casts range from the mundane to the fantastic, not the least of which are silver and even precious opal.

One way to introduce your child to this process is to make a fossil cast of your own. If you haven't any spare precious opal don't worry—plaster of Paris will do nicely. First, gather the materials listed below, then have your son or daughter choose what will be preserved for posterity—perhaps a shell, a simple plastic dinosaur figure, or even the footprint of the family dog or cat.

Materials:

Modeling clay
Plaster of Paris
Water
An empty coffee can

An old spoon
A 4-inch by 12-inch strip of heavy paper or thin cardboard
Tape
Newspapers

Instructions:

1. Put a couple of sheets of newspaper on a tabletop or the floor.
2. Form the modeling clay into a ball that measures about three inches across when flattened. Place the clay on the newspaper. Take the item to be preserved and press it into the clay. Make a deep, clear impression, then remove the item.
3. Wrap the strip of paper or cardboard around the edge of the clay to form a tight ring. Secure the ends with tape.
4. In the coffee can, prepare the plaster of Paris according to the directions on the package. Pour the plaster onto the clay, covering it completely.
5. Let the plaster dry (it will take at least three hours). Remove the paper ring and clay to reveal the finished plaster cast.

Fossils may also form through the mineralization of an animal's remains. For example, if a creature dies in or near still water, or if it is swept away in a flood, its body may be covered by mud that can eventually harden, locking the carcass (bones and teeth, most likely) inside. This sort of rapid burial is critical to fossilization. Animal bones are not solid; they are riddled with tiny pores. The bones are made up of two main elements: apatite, a mineral that makes bones hard, and collagen, a protein that makes bones resilient. Over millions of years, the collagen breaks down and mineral-bearing water seeps in. Mineral deposits eventually replace the original bone, which is effectively turned to stone.

Fossils may also form in which some of the original material remains intact, but as a rule, only bones and teeth are preserved. Soft body parts such as the brain, heart, and skin decay. Muscles also disintegrate, but they often leave behind marks on the bones to which they were attached. Scientists are left with only a few clues and a lot of questions.

Although not a part of the animal proper, another important fossil form is the trace fossil. This includes coprolites (fossilized dung), skin impressions, tracks, and anything else a creature may have left behind. Once again, you can demonstrate to your child how trace fossils are made by whipping up a batch of plaster of Paris.

Materials:

Newspaper
Plaster of Paris
An old shallow baking pan with a 1-inch rim
Heavy cardboard
Scissors
A pen
A long shoestring

Instructions:

1. First, have your child draw and cut out a dinosaur footprint of his or her own design from very heavy cardboard. The print should be a little larger than your youngster's own foot.
2. Have your youngster place his or her foot on the dinosaur print. With the pen make a small mark on the cardboard on either side of his or her foot. Poke holes through each mark with the scissors, string the shoelace through, and tie the print to your youngster's foot as if it were a shoe.

3. Lay down some sheets of newspaper on the floor and place the baking pan on top. Mix the plaster of Paris according to the directions on the package. Pour a layer about a half-inch deep into the baking pan. Allow it to thicken slightly. Tell your child to pretend the plaster is thick mud at the edge of prehistoric river.

4. While holding his or her hand for support, have your youngster step into the plaster. When your little "dinosaur" removes her or his foot, a well-defined footprint will be left behind and will soon dry and harden.

WHAT DO WE LEARN FROM FOSSILS?

With tremendous luck, the remains of a plant or animal may fossilize. With more luck, such processes as weathering and erosion will wear down the rock to expose the remains. Good fortune must hold even further if the fossil is to catch the eye of a paleontologist before it, too, is worn away. Those that survive, no matter how small, are true treasures of the earth.

Fossils are unique storehouses of information. The level of rock in which they are found provide clues as to when and where the animal lived. From the size of the bones we can determine the size and weight of the animal. Teeth are clues to what kind of food it ate. The dimensions of internal cavities in the skull may reveal the size and shape of the brain, which helps us determine how intelligent the creature may have been. The proportions of eye sockets are an indication of the animal's visual capability. Even a dinosaur's health can be studied. One fossil hadrosaur showed evidence of a cancerous bone tumor.

Fossilized footprints hint at how their maker walked and at what speed, whether it traveled in herds or alone, and if it moved on two feet or four. (Of course, this brings to mind an image of a very tiny dinosaur with tremendously large feet! Fossil evidence is always subject to interpretation.) A series of tracks was discovered in Australia that had been made by 130 large dinosaurs traveling at about five miles per hour. Another set of footprints reveals why these animals were in a hurry: they were being followed by a meat-eater. One can almost imagine the scene as it was those many millions of years ago.

We also learn from what we *don't* see in the tracks. We can assume that dinosaurs didn't drag their tails, because no tail marks have ever been found. One set of prints discovered in the eastern United States puzzled scientists at first. They were made by a dinosaur that touched the ground only with its front toes. What was it doing? It appears that the beast was swimming, using its toes to push along the bottom.

> **With your child** : Create your own "short term fossils" by burying a variety of objects three different ways to investigate how each item is affected. Collect three complete sets of items. Each set could include a chicken bone, a cotton sock, a shell, an egg, and a flower. Bury one set in dry sand, bury the other two separately in heavy soil. Thoroughly water the soil over one set and leave the other dry. Mark each area so that you can retrieve the items later. After a month or so, help your youngster dig up the "fossils" and see if and how each set was altered.

The First Dinosaur Hunters

More than 1,700 years ago, Chinese scholars noted the discovery of huge animal bones, which they believed were the remains of dragons. A Sioux legend tells of huge serpents that, when struck by lightning, burrowed into the ground to die. Their huge bones finally surfaced and supposedly littered the badlands. In the late 1600s, a drawing of an unusually large bone appeared in the book *The Natural History of Oxfordshire* by Robert Plot. The bone was then identified as that of a giant elephant. Nearly two hundred years later, new discoveries led scientists to believe that the bones in question did not belong to any known creatures. They were the remains of unfamiliar, even frightening, reptiles.

The intellectual stage had to be set, however, before the world could accept the existence of such beasts. Most people thought the earth wasn't much more than six thousand years old. The discovery of a magnificent lifeform that obviously no longer walked the planet was a tough pill to swallow. It would have been impossible if not for the work of scientists like French biologist Georges Cuvier, the father of comparative anatomy. He was so skilled that he could often identify a creature from a single bone. Cuvier was well respected, and when he suggested the concept of extinction during the nineteenth century, his theory met with little resistance.

In 1790, Scottish geologist James Hutton, published a book called *The Theory of the Earth.* He proposed that the formation and the eventual wearing away of mountains took a great deal of time—thousands, perhaps millions, of years. He proposed that the earth was much older than anyone had suspected. (The idea didn't catch on right away, but it was picked up and reintroduced in 1830 by geologist Charles Lyell.) With such things considered, it was quite possible for an ancient form of life to have existed and disappeared long before humans claimed the earth. The time was right for the dawning of the new age of the dinosaurs.

We will probably never know when the first dinosaur bones were uncovered by curious humans. The first to be recognized as remains of a new species were found in England in 1822 by British doctor Gideon Mantell. According to legend, Dr. Mantell's wife, Mary Ann, took an afternoon walk on a British lane. She is said to have discovered a most unusual fossil tooth embedded in stone and carried it back to show her husband. Some historians claim that the romantic tale is inaccurate, and that is was another collector who sent the specimen to Mantell. Regardless of how he came by it, Mantell sent the tooth to Cuvier, who misidentified it as the tooth of a rhino. Unconvinced, Mantell investigated further. A colleague noticed a similarity between the fossil tooth and the teeth of a Central American iguana. Mantell persevered and was able to convince others of the nature of the specimen, and the new creature was dubbed *Iguanodon.* When speculating about the appearance of the creature in life, however, Dr. Mantell was wide of the mark. He pictured the beast much like a huge, quadrupedal lizard. He was also a little slow in formally announcing his find to the scientific world.

In 1818 some teeth, ribs, and other bones were unearthed in England by anatomist William Buckland. These remains were the first fossils *publicly* recognized in 1824 as being those of a new kind of creature—a fierce meat-eater that came to be called *Megalosaurus.* Mantell described *Iguanodon* soon after, and in 1833 he added a third dinosaur, *Hylaeosaurus* (hy-LEE-oh-SAWR-us), to the growing ranks of mysterious giant reptiles.

The first important American fossils included a partial skeleton of a *Hadrosaurus* found in New Jersey in 1858. It was not long before the race to uncover and describe new species began in earnest.

The Bone Wars

In 1838 Charles Lyell combined three Greek words to create the name *paleontology,* "the science of ancient being," and since then paleontologists have revolutionized our view of the world. It is well beyond the scope of this book to acknowledge all or even a reasonable number of the men and women who have contributed and continue to contribute to this science. John Noble Wilford's wonderful book *The Riddle of the Dinosaur* gives a detailed and delightful history if you care to explore further. Nevertheless, I would like to briefly mention several paleontologists who are greatly responsible for our modern body of knowledge.

Two American scientists stand out, and their rivalry is a colorful chapter in the history of the field. To Edward Drinker Cope and Othniel Charles (O. C.) Marsh, the North American West proved to be a bottomless cache of dinosaur fossils. As with many paleontologists, both men were attracted to the study of fossils early in life. As a child, Marsh collected fossils exposed when the Erie Canal was widened. Cope was a born naturalist. On family outings he would entertain himself by exploring the arca and sketching the fauna. By the late 1800s both men had established themselves in the scientific community. Each did competent field work, Cope certainly the better of the two, but eventually they hired teams of fossil hunters and field hands to search for new finds.

These hunters were part scientist, part detective, all adventurer. They braved harsh weather, floods, lack of transportation, loneliness, cave-ins, and on occasion, hostile Indians. The rush to find the most and grandest fossils and to be the first to describe new species led both sides to resort to questionable methods. The rivalry was eventually reduced to name-calling that culminated in spiteful accusatory articles each scientist wrote about the other. Nevertheless, the Bone Wars were very productive. Before they began, only nine North American dinosaur species were known. We have Cope and Marsh to thank for raising that number to more than one hundred. In fact, together, the two men were responsible for describing more than 1,700 fossil vertebrates of North America.

The Find at Flaming Cliffs

In April 1922, Roy Chapman Andrews set out into the Gobi Desert to search for the bones of our human ancestors. Under the title of the Central Asiatic Expedition, 40 men endured scorching heat, choking dust storms, bandits, invading armies, and suspicious government officials who believed the group was actually in search of gold or oil. There were five expeditions altogether. The first (to an area called Flaming Cliffs) produced the remains of a new species christened *Protoceratops andrewsi*

in honor of Andrews. The following year, the second expedition returned
to Flaming Cliffs, and on July 13, 1923, Andrews and his companions
discovered something in the brick-red sands that would forever ensure
their place in history—dinosaur eggs! The eight-inch-long, oval-shaped
Protoceratops eggs rested in a spiral pattern that suggest the mother
either moved around the nest as she laid her eggs, or positioned them
after they were laid.

Other new species were uncovered on that expedition, including *Velociraptor, Oviraptor, Pinacosaurus* (an armored dinosaur), and *Saurornithoides,* as well as the tiny skull of a Cretaceous mammal. On later
forays into the Gobi Desert, Andrews and his colleagues continued to
unearth valuable specimens, but political unrest in Mongolia finally made
such exploration too dangerous, and the expeditions were discontinued.

Andrews went on to write several books about his adventures, and
he won a special place in the hearts of young would-be adventurers.
He was instrumental in promoting the nation's fascination with dinosaurs
and natural history in general, and many modern paleontologists were
first introduced to the science through the exploits of Roy Chapman
Andrews.

Dinosaurs on Ice

Many, but not all, modern paleontologists were bitten by the dinosaur
bug early in life. Dr. Edwin Colbert, whose name is synonymous with
modern paleontology, first became interested in the study of fossils in
college, but his interest was not necessarily geared toward fossil reptiles.
Upon completion of his studies he joined the staff at the American
Museum of Natural History in New York. As fate would have it, the
curator of reptiles retired in 1942, and Colbert took over the position.

When pressed to choose those contributions he feels were most important, he first mentions Dinosaur Quarry at Ghost Ranch, New Mexico.
There, in the summer of 1947, Colbert and his assistant, George
Whitaker, unearthed the remains of more than a dozen individual *Coelophysis,* a primitive Triassic dinosaur first described by Edward Drinker
Cope in 1887. One skeleton held a most unusual puzzle: tiny bones of a
juvenile *Coelophysis* were found within the body cavity of an adult. Was
this evidence of a creature capable of live birth? Far from it. Rather, it
seems that *Coelophysis* was, at least at times, cannibalistic and not adverse to gobbling down its own young.

Antarctica is not the sort of place one would expect to find prehistoric reptiles, but in 1969 Dr. Colbert and paleontologist Jim Jensen* journeyed to the slopes of the Transantarctic Mountains, 350 miles from the South Pole. There, in Earth's harshest environment, they uncovered the bones and skull of *Lystrosaurus,* a small therapsid that predated the age of the dinosaurs. This animal had also been discovered in Africa. Here was strong evidence that the two land masses were once linked, thus reinforcing the theory of continental drift. It would not be too long before dinosaur fossils (those of an ankylosaurid) would also be found on James Ross Island in Antarctica.

Colbert retired from the American Museum in 1970, having opened many doors through his research, and his influence is still felt in all areas of paleontology.

A New Breed

Over the past 20 years, the image of the dinosaur has changed dramatically. Yale paleontologist Dr. John Ostrom has been instrumental in establishing this new image. His contributions to the field are legion. Dinosaurs were not his first fascination, however. Like many young people, Ostrom found baseball more to his liking than science, but that was to change, thanks to a remarkable and inspiring ninth-grade science teacher, Gretchen Pentecost. "She opened all the doors for me," says Ostrom. "She demonstrated things in that classroom . . . asked questions . . . and made me aware of what a fantastic world this is. Since that year I have been science-oriented." Paleontology, however, was still waiting in the wings. Ostrom planned to become a medical doctor until he picked up a book by George Baylord Simpson, *The Meaning of Evolution.* "I read the whole thing in one night but it wasn't enough. I had to know more, so I wrote to the author." Ostrom eventually studied with Simpson and through him met Edwin Colbert, who, according to Ostrom, "encouraged me to think in terms of dinosaurs as well as mammals."

Ostrom's subsequent work has, among other things, established a strong case for a dinosaur-bird link. With one find in particular, a most

*Jim Jensen began collecting fossils at the age of ten and turned his fascination into a lifelong pursuit. Until 1983, he was the curator of the vertebrate paleontology Research Laboratory at Brigham Young University. Known as "Dinosaur Jim," he is responsible for the discovery of the remains of two dinosaurs that may be among the largest to march across the face of the earth—*Supersaurus* and *Ultrasaurus.*

unusual claw, he drastically altered the once widespread perception of dinosaurs as slow, dim-witted animals.

It was in 1964 in Montana hill country that Ostrom and his assistant, Grant E. Meyer, chanced upon a clawed hand rising from the solid ground. They had not planned to dig that day, so the proper tools had been left behind. Both men were so excited that they did the best they could with jackknives and fingernails. They managed to uncover more of the hand and several sharp, jagged-edged teeth. This creature was definitely a meat-eater. Ostrom and Meyer continued their work the following day (with more serious tools) and soon uncovered one of the animal's feet, which proved to be startlingly unlike that of other carnivores. The inner toe ended in a frightful sickle-shaped claw. The claw was obviously a weapon, one that could be used by an agile predator that leapt and slashed at its prey—hardly the image of a cold-blooded, sluggish reptile. The amazing creature would be introduced to the world as *Deinonychus,* or "terrible claw."

Is *Deinonychus* proof that the dinosaurs were warm-blooded? Ostrom himself does not necessarily think so. He explains, "I think [warm-bloodedness] is an overly simplistic expression of how these animals operated. There is no reason to believe that they all operated in the same way. Not all mammals are truly "warm-blooded." There are grades. I think the same is true of the dinosaurs. I suspect that very few approached anything like the mammal or bird level of thermoregulation."

Still, the tide had shifted and a new, vibrant dinosaur entered the picture. But does Ostrom consider this find the greatest of his achievements? "If I have awakened the curiosity of any of my students," he says, "that's the best."

The Superiority of Dinosaurs

If John Ostrom introduced the concept of lively dinosaurs, one of Ostrom's students, Robert T. Bakker, Adjunct Curator of Paleontology at the University of Colorado Museum, brought it center stage. Bakker's interest in dinosaurs was piqued in the fourth grade. He saw the mighty beasts in what he describes as a wonderfully illustrated article in *Life* magazine, and he was hooked. "It hit me all of a sudden," he notes. "It was a dramatic discovery, not only of the idea of dinosaurs, but of all that history."

Although his parents were convinced that his passion would fade, they were proved wrong. As a youngster he looked forward to biannual pilgrimages with his mother to the American Museum of Natural History in New York. He never accepted, however, the representations of dinosaurs as sprawling, lethargic reptiles, and he has since devoted his career to painting a far different picture.

Bakker spent his undergraduate years at Yale and went on to obtain a doctorate at Harvard. During his more than 15 expeditions into the American West, he has brought to light what may be the largest member of the allosaur family, the Jurassic dinosaur: *Epanterias*, (eh-pan-TAYR-ee-us), a 50-foot-long, four-ton predator that probably rivaled *Tyrannosaurus rex* in ferocity, and a little plant-eater no more than six feet long from nose to tail called *Drinker nisti*. Also to his credit are the discoveries of 11 new species of early mammal (including a creature affectionately known as the 'mutant ninja chipmunk'). From the very beginning, Bakker has championed the concept of warm-blooded, fast-moving, capable dinosaurs. A fine artist as well, he depicts these creatures as colorful, perhaps beautifully patterned animals. Bakker's enthusiasm for the prehistoric world is evident in his spirited approach to every aspect of paleontology: "It's a wonderful smorgasbord of animals, geology, history, chemistry . . . all sorts of great things."

Bakker's provocative ideas (for example, his suggestion that some sauropods may have given live birth) have at times attracted criticism, but he considers his willingness to take a chance as being in his favor. His pioneering nature adds further zest to an already vigorous science.

Family Life

You can often find fossils for sale in rock shops, but John R. Horner, curator of paleontology at the Museum of the Rockies in Bozeman, Montana, found more than he bargained for when he stopped at a rock shop in Bynum, Montana, in 1978. Horner (on vacation from the musuem at Princeton University) and his associate, science teacher Bob Makela, had stopped by the shop at the urging of another paleontologist. The fossils Horner saw seemed fairly commonplace until the store's owner, Marion Branvold, presented him with a coffee can that held a few tiny bones. The fossils may have been small, but their importance would turn out to monumental. They were the bones of baby duckbilled dinosaurs.

Like many paleontologists, John Horner had become captivated by dinosaurs at a very young age, finding his first dinosaur bone in Montana when he was eight years old. The remarkable bones in the coffee can had been unearthed only about 30 miles from the site of his first discovery. After securing permission from the owner of the property where Branvold had found the tiny fossil bones, Horner and Makela were soon digging into a formation of gray-green mudstone. They uncovered the bones of some 15 baby duckbills—and something else. It seems that in life the young dinosaurs had been restricted to a six-foot-wide by three-foot-deep bowl-shaped cavity in the earth, a cavity that could be a nest! These were the first baby dinosaurs ever found in a nest, and the obvious wear on their teeth led Horner to an astonishing conclusion: these youngsters were being cared for by one or both parents.

The surprise did not end there. It appeared that this duckbill was of an unknown species, one that was appropriately named *Maiasaura,* or "good mother lizard." This nest was only the tip of the iceberg. To date, Horner has uncovered hundreds of nests, eggs, eggshells, embryos, hatchlings, juveniles, and even parents. It has become apparent that the Maiasaur gathered on upland plains by the hundreds, away from predator-filled lowlands, to lay their eggs and raise their young, a practice unheard of in the world of modern reptiles.

The remains of two other species of dinosaur and their eggs have also been found in that area. The site has offered a bounty of information about the social behavior of certain dinosaurs, and John Horner has shed light on an aspect of the dinosaur world that had for years been subject only to speculation.

TOMORROW'S DINOSAUR HUNTERS

Dinosaurs are as intriguing as any life form that has developed since. At any given time there are thousands of people all around the world that are working to lift the veil of mystery that surrounds these marvelous beasts. There is so much work yet to be done, and it is from the ranks of today's eager dinosaur fans that tomorrow's paleontologists will step forth. How can one best encourage his or her child if they have an interest in a scientific field? Dr. John Ostrom offered some sound advice: "I think youngsters should be encouraged to learn about anything that interests them . . . to seek answers, to pursue and investigate whatever questions come into their minds, be it science or Shakespeare. What I have learned is that you are likely to do best in what you enjoy the most." With that in mind, it's time to get "into the field" and start exploring the new age of dinosaurs with your child.

PART TWO

Exploring the New Age of Dinosaurs with Your Child

8

A Visit to the Museum

Less than two hundred years ago, people didn't realize that dinosaurs existed. Today, the great beasts are so familiar that it is hard to believe they no longer walk the earth. In a way, they still do. Across the continent there are hundreds of pockets of prehistoric life. As if frozen in time, mounted fossils, casts, reconstructions, and models of dinosaurs and other prehistoric creatures saunter, stroll, and stride through hundreds of natural history museums and parks. If a picture is worth a thousand words, then a visit to one of these sites is worth volumes! Why not designate a special "dinosaur day" centered on an expedition that will bring your youngster face-to-face with a dinosaur? (If there isn't a park or museum close by, you might consider making such a visit part of the family vacation plans.)

You'll need to do a little preparation. Call to find out what exhibits are featured at your nearest museum (there may also be special tours or programs that the entire family will enjoy). Visit the library and help your child prepare a fact file on the creature or creatures you will see.

One way to increase the value of your youngster's visit is to give her or him an idea of how much effort is involved in preparing a fossil or model for display. There are many varieties of fossil kits on the market designed for children to assemble. Depending on your child's age, you may want to make the project tougher by doing it without instructions, using only the picture of the animal as a guide. For an even greater challenge, remove a piece or two ahead of time. Ask your child to decide what the missing bone is and draw a picture of it, then compare the drawing to the actual piece. If you cannot find a kit, create a simple puzzle by copying a picture of a dinosaur skeleton from a book. Glue the copy to thin cardboard, then cut it apart. You needn't separate each bone; large sections such as the rib cage, the spine, and limb bones will do. When your youngster has completed the model or reassembled the cut-outs, explain that the paleontologist's reconstructions on view in the museum also had to be put together like pieces of a difficult puzzle.

GATHERING THE PIECES

Once a fossil has been uncovered, it must be carefully prepared for its trip to the laboratory for study. First it is labeled and photographed or sketched in place. The position of the remains and the properties of the rock in which it is found often yield clues to how the animal lived or died. This can be of critical importance in reconstruction. If small fossils appear cracked or crumbly, they are hardened by soaking them with glue or shellac, then wrapped in tissue and stored in protective boxes or crates. Often they are simply transported within the large chunks of rock they were found in, to be removed at a more convenient time.

Large fossils can be very difficult to extract from their stony graves. First, any layers of rock above the fossil are removed with picks, hammers, shovels, and sometimes explosives. As the diggers get closer to the bones, they use chisels, knives, brushes, and even fingernails until at least half of the bone is uncovered. The exposed portion of the find is then covered with wet tissue paper to prevent sticking, and is encased in foam or, more often, a protective jacket of burlap strips soaked in wet plaster (not unlike the cast created to protect a human's broken bone). Finally, the rock beneath the bone is tunneled away. Once the fossil has been turned over and plastered on the opposite side, it is ready to be moved. This isn't easy. Large fossils can be so heavy that moving them can put a bulldozer to the test. This painstaking process may take months or several digging seasons.

PUTTING THE PIECES TOGETHER

If gathering the pieces takes months, putting them together may take years! In the lab, technicians saw off the casts, or jackets, then remove every trace of rock and clean each specimen with delicate instruments and chemicals. When necessary, they repair cracked, chipped, or broken fossils. Scientists catalog, photograph, study, and describe every bone.

They use many leads to help them reconstruct the skeleton, such as information from the original find, marks on the bone that indicate where muscles and cartilage were attached, and comparisons with modern animals. Common sense comes in handy, too. Since complete skeletons are rarely found, the reconstructions in museums are often put together from the bones of several individuals. Sometimes it's necessary to manufacture artificial bones to replace missing ones. Bones of newborns or juveniles (as well as skulls of adults) are fairly delicate and often crushed during the fossilization process. For example, only one known *Apatosaurus* skull has ever been discovered. The exhibits in museums are usually not made up entirely of bone or mineralized bone. Rather, displays may be casts or models made from the original fossils using fiberglass, plaster, epoxy, and even *papier-mâché*. In fact, you and your child could create your own dinosaur displays and be the first on your block to open your own museum!

BUILDING A DINOSAUR

Translated from French, *papier-mâché* means "chewed paper." It's not as bad as it sounds, and one benefit of this method of model-building is that it's easy to clean up afterward.

Materials:

A large empty coffee can or the bottom three-quarters of a gallon-size plastic milk container
Fine-mesh chicken wire
String, thin wire, or masking tape
Wire clippers
Newspapers
Glue
Flour
Water
Rubber gloves (optional)

Instructions:

1. First, you and your child must choose the dinosaur you will create. *Apatosaurus* is not too difficult for a start. The base for the model is

shaped from chicken wire. You may come up with variations of your own, but here are the basics for a two-foot-long sauropod.

2. Start with the body. Cut out enough chicken wire to create a cylinder eight inches long and four inches in diameter. Secure it lengthwise with wire, string, or masking tape.

3. Once this is complete, push in both ends to form a slightly rounded shape. This is the dinosaur's body.

4. To make the neck and head, cut out another piece of chicken wire to form an eight-inch-long cylinder that is about three inches in diameter. Secure one end of the neck to one end of the body. Working from that end outward, gently squeeze the neck down until it narrows to about an inch in diameter at the opposite end. Curve the last inch or so down to serve as the head.

5. Repeat step 4 at the other end of the dinosaur's body to form the tail.

6. The legs are made with cylinders, each two inches long. For the forelegs, the cylinders should be three quarters of an inch in diameter. For the hind legs, they should be one inch in diameter.

7. Now, the artistry is in adding the dinosaur's "skin." In a coffee can, mix one part flour to two parts water to form a thin paste.

8. Tear several dozen long strips (about an inch wide) from the newspaper. Dip one strip into the paste to coat it, then lay it over the wire frame. Repeat with another strip, then another, layering the strips one at a time to build up the dinosaur. To create the animal's muscular upper thigh, wad up a little newspaper. Position the wad, then layer coated strips over it to hold it in place.

9. Make the end of *Apatosaurus*'s tail by dipping a wide strip of paper into the paste. Allow the excess fluid to drip off, then roll the paper in your hands to form a slender roll. Attach that to the tail end of the chicken wire and hold it in place with additional strips of coated paper.

10. Once the model is completed, give it a day or so to dry fully. A coat of poster paint will add the finishing touches to your model. Encourage your child to experiment with stripes or patterns. Once you both get the hang of *papier-mâché*, you can craft an entire prehistoric zoo filled with crested, spiked, and horned dinosaurs. Be creative! Cut plates out of cardboard using toothpicks as a base for spikes, horns, or scary-looking teeth.

SET THE SCENE

More and more museums incorporate exhibits of dinosaur models shown in the animal's original habitat. Your child can build a similar presentation in a shoebox. Once again, you will find most of the materials you need around the house or in the yard.

Materials:
A shoe box with lid
Pencil
White paper
Scissors
Glue
Sand or soil
Pebbles
A small mirror
Plastic dinosaur figures
Modeling clay
Colored construction paper
Nature magazines with pictures of dinosaurs
Light cardboard
String
3 × 5 index cards

Instructions:

1. Start by having your youngster draw the background of his dinosaur scene directly on one inner wall of the shoe box, then cut a large viewing window in the opposite wall. The background can also be drawn on a separate sheet of white paper which is then cut to size and glued into the box.

2. Layer sand or soil in the bottom of the box and add a few pebbles. Put a small hand mirror in one spot and surround it with a little sand to create a "pool" of water.

3. Use plastic dinosaur figures to populate the scene. Your child can also model creatures out of clay, draw and cut dinosaurs and plants out of construction paper, or cut pictures out of a magazine. For the latter, glue the pictures to pieces of light cardboard and attach a cardboard support in back so the dinosaurs will stand up.

4. Add variety. Try hanging a pterosaur by a string from the lid so it appears to be gliding through the air when the lid is placed on top of the box.

5. To make sure the setting is accurate, use dinosaurs and plants that existed simultaneously. Remind your child that there were no flowering trees in the Triassic and no grassy fields in the Jurassic.

6. When the diorama is complete, write the time period and the dinosaurs depicted on a 3 × 5 card and tape it to the side of the box. Now try making a different exhibit for each period. Or how about a dinosaur nursery or an underwater scene?

Models and dioramas aren't the only exhibits your child can put together for home display. Here's a chance to show off the handcrafted fossils described in the previous chapter and the fossil collection we'll discuss in the next. For variety, don't rule out making a poster, collage, or mobile. You both will probably get further inspiration when you tour your local museum.

VISIT THE SOURCE

When you visit the museum or park, remember that you are likely to be doing a lot of walking, so dress comfortably. Don't forget a drawing pad and a "guidebook" such as *The Dinosaur Encyclopedia* by Dr. Michael

Benton to help answer questions that come up. Not all museums have restaurant facilities, so you may want to bring a small "snack pak" along for yourself and each child. Also, planning a picnic on the museum grounds (if permitted) can add to the enjoyment of the day. The following is a small sampling of major museums and parks across the country to give you an idea of what is available. See Appendix 1 for addresses and phone numbers of these and other attractions.

National Museum of Natural History/ Natural Museum of Man

You can introduce your youngster to a dinosaur before you even set foot in this museum at our nation's capital. Across from the entrance on the National Mall, a life-sized model of a *Triceratops*, affectionately known as Uncle Beazley, stoops so that children can climb onto its back. Inside the museum, the dinosaurs represented (either fully mounted or in slab mounts) include *Camarasaurus, Ceratosaurus, Diplodocus, Heterodontosaurus, Maiasaura, Stegosaurus,* and *Triceratops.* In the central gallery there is a myriad of Mesozoic marvels such as the remains of a gigantic 80-foot-long *Diplodocus* discovered in Utah that took a year to remove from the ground and seven years to reconstruct; life-sized models of dinosaurs in their native habitats; casts of dinosaur eggs; and a cast of an *Archaeopteryx* fossil. A life-sized replica of *Quetzalcoatlus,* the largest known winged creature ever to have lived, is suspended above. Other fossil creatures of prehistory grace the balconies that overlook the dinosaur gallery.

The Naturalist's Center gives children ages 12 and up the opportunity for hand-on research. Using scientific instruments, they can examine specimens of rock, a bit of a *Triceratops* horn, and other materials. Younger children will enjoy the Discovery Room, where a variety of interesting specimens can be touched and examined.

This museum is open every day of the year with the exception of Christmas Day, and there is no admission fee. Hours are usually 10 A.M. to 5:30 P.M. (longer in the spring and summer). No public parking facility is available, but there are several commercial lots in the area. You may want to leave the car at home or at your hotel and just ride the Metrorail. The museum shop offers books and souvenirs and a cafeteria is on the premises.

Dinosaur State Park

About 185 MYA this area, just south of what is now Hartford, Connecticut, was covered by a huge lake and ringed by a maze of mudflats. Dinosaurs and other prehistoric creatures trekked daily through the thick mud, leaving behind hundreds of tracks. You can gaze upon those tracks, frozen in time, as if they were left only yesterday. In 1966, the land was being cleared for a state building project when a sharp-eyed bulldozer operator uncovered the unsual footprints and realized they were quite special. Local scientists soon discovered some 1,500 tracks, which were later reburied in order to preserve them. In 1967 an additional 500 tracks were uncovered. Protected by a 122-foot geodesic dome, these tracks are the park's central attraction. Some tracks were left by *Coelophysis,* for which a comparatively great number of fossil remains have been uncovered. In contrast, the park's "star," a dinosaur called *Eubrontes,* or "true thunder," is known only by the tracks found in this park (and similar tracks found in Germany). This creature was named for the fact that it probably shook the ground as it walked. The footprints, 10 to 16 inches long with a span of about 4 feet between each print, were thought to have been made by a 20-foot-long, 8-foot-tail, 3-toed carnosaur similar to the meat-eater known as *Dilophosaurus* ("two-crested lizard"). A replica of this beast stalks the grounds of the park. Another set of tracks has also gained a lot of attention. These tracks seem to have been left by a large dinosaur that was swimming in shallow water at the time, pushing off the lake bottom with its toes.

Facilities at the dome include a bookstore, an auditorium for lectures and films, the exhibit hall, and the trackway. A boardwalk extends over the trackway. Lighting designed to highlight detail gives an excellent view of a large section of footprints. Beyond the central building winds a mile of nature trails where picnic tables are available. Dinosaur State Park also offers a unique opportunity for the children. If you bring along 10 pounds of plaster of Paris, ¼ cup of cooking oil, and a few old rags, your child can make his or her own cast of a *Eubrontes* footprint to take home. (What a unique addition that would be to your youngster's personal museum!)

The park is open daily (except New Year's Day, Thanksgiving Day, and Christmas Day) from 9:00 A.M. to 4:30 P.M. and there is an admission charge. The exhibit center is closed on Mondays, and the casting area is open from May through October.

The Field Museum of Natural History

Chicago's Field Museum is home to the first dinosaur skeleton mounted with no visibile supports. This *Albertosaurus* towers over a fallen *Lambeosaurus*. There's no shortage of dinosaurs here. Those on display include *Apatosaurus, Edmontosaurus, Protoceratops,* and a host of others along with many Mesozoic reptiles, prehistoric mammals, birds, and fish.

The Field Museum is open 9:00 A.M. to 5:00 P.M. daily except New Year's Day, Thanksgiving Day, and Christmas Day. There is usually an admission fee, but on Thursday entry is free to all. You'll find several small shopping areas here, a museum store, and several food services.

The Royal Tyrrell Museum of Palaeontology

Western Canada is famous for its dinosaurs, and the town of Drumheller in Alberta is a storehouse of dinosaur lore. Millions of years ago, the surrounding land was a series of floodplains and deltas formed by rivers flowing east to a warm, inland sea. Today it is the location of the largest museum display of dinosaurs in the world—the Royal Tyrrell Museum of Palaeontology in the badlands a little west of Drumheller. More than 30 complete dinosaurs are on display as well as prehistoric reptiles, mammals, sailbacked amphibians, and even a forest of plants related to ancient species that grew in Alberta during the time of the dinosaurs.

In 1884, Joseph Tyrrell discovered the skull of an *Albertosaurus* in this area, the first of the species ever found. To this day the site is yielding a wealth of remarkable fossils. In the main preparation lab you and your child can observe the scientists at work preparing specimens. Special programs, hands-on displays (signs let you know when you can touch), and computer simulations add to the excitement.

In the summer the museum hours are from 9:00 A.M. to 9:00 P.M. daily. In winter the doors close at 5:00 P.M. and the museum is closed on Mondays. There is no admission charge but donations are encouraged. Picnic areas, a cafeteria, a bookstore, and a gift shop are available for your convenience. If you are in the area for a few days you can also visit the nearby Drumheller Dinosaur and Fossil Museum and the Tyrrell Museum Field Station in Dinosaur Provincial Park.

Dinosaur National Monument

If your family likes the great outdoors, Dinosaur National Monument is the perfect place for a "dinosaur oriented" vacation. The quarry and 200,000 acres of surrounding land were declared a national monument in 1915 in an effort to protect the area, which has yielded some of the finest fossils in the world, including skulls, near-complete skeletons, and the remains of young dinosaurs. This treasure trove of dinosaur fossils was identified in 1909 by fossil hunter Earl Douglass of the Carnegie Museum. The first discovery revealed was the remains of an *Apatosaurus,* to date the most complete ever discovered. Today the park lies across the border between Utah and Colorado (its mailing address is in Utah), but between 145 and 135 MYA this land was located on the western shore of a great inland sea. The focus of the museum, the Dinosaur Quarry, is an ancient sandbar or riverbed that became the final resting place of hundreds of Mesozoic animals, including a great many sauropods. Over millions of years it was buried, then raised once again. The quarry forms the rear wall of the building and holds some 2,000 fossils. The creatures represented include *Apatosaurus, Diplodocus, Camarasaurus, Stegosaurus* (including a juvenile), and the fierce meat-eaters *Allosaurus* and *Ceratosaurus.* The remains of turtles, clams, and even crocodiles give credence to the supposed nature of the area during the age of reptiles. In general, between April and October, you can watch paleontologists in their painstaking efforts to coax the fossils from the stone. The remains are not necessarily being removed. In fact, the lowest layer will remain intact.

Dinosaurs are the main attraction here, but there's plenty to do in the park, including hiking, scenic drives, boating, fishing (you'll need a permit), guided river trips, and camping. Fossils are on exhibit only at Dinosaur Quarry, but if your child is in grade four, five, or six, he or she is welcome at the Kid's Hut, where park rangers conduct activities to help youngsters understand the nature of the park as it is today. Check the schedule for these one-hour sessions because you need to sign up at the Quarry ahead of time.

The visitor's center near the town of (what else?) Dinosaur, Colorado, can acquaint you with the park facilities and activities. The park is open everyday in the summer and on weekdays only in the winter. You can drive directly to the Dinosaur Quarry but parking is limited. During the busiest times, it's best to leave your car in the main parking area and take the free shuttle to the museum.

The Fort Worth Museum of Science and History

If you are near Fort Worth, Texas, set aside a whole day to explore this museum. Under the 80-foot dome of the Omni Theatre you are treated to an incredible view of the world. Then, in the Noble Planetarium, you can get a peek at the rest of the universe. But what about dinosaurs? You'll find them in the Rocks and Fossils room. Centered around a pair of dinosaurs locked in combat, the permanent collection includes a wide variety of meteorites and fossils.

While the museum is open every day of the week, hours vary. There is an admission charge but children under four are free. You will need to obtain tickets to visit the theatre or planetarium. You and your youngster can browse for souvenirs in the museum store or take a break at the courtyard cafe.

The Natural History Museum of Los Angeles County

As you walk through the entry doors of L.A.'s Natural History Museum, you are greeted by the remarkable sight of a *Camptosaurus* struggling to avoid an attacking *Allosaurus.* This museum, the third largest of its kind in the United States, has much to offer the dinosaur enthusiast. *Tyrannosaurus rex* is represented by one of the finest skulls on display anywhere. In the Olympics Gallery you can view fossils and casts of such creatures as *Mamenchisaurus* and *Triceratops* as well as the terror of the seas, the mosasaur, with soaring pterosaurs to round everything out.

There is plenty of fun for the kids in the Discovery Center which offers, among other activities, the opportunity to make fossil rubbings from a special rock wall. The motto here is look and please touch.

With the exception of New Year's Day, Thanksgiving Day, and Christmas Day, the museum is open from 10:00 A.M. to 5:00 P.M. Tuesday through Sunday. The hours for the Discovery Center are 11:00 A.M. to 3:00 P.M. There is an admission charge but children under five are free, and admission on the first Tuesday of the every month is free to everyone! Facilities include an indoor/outdoor cafeteria that is open until 4:00 P.M., an Ethnic Arts shop, a bookstore, and the Dinosaur Shop, which carries books, games, and educational materials. The Discovery Center also offers dinosaur birthday parties for youngsters.

Knott's Berry Farm

For a real change of pace, you may want to treat your child to a visit to one of the dinosaur theme parks that are springing up around the nation. If you are in the Los Angeles area, Knott's Berry Farm offers Kingdom of the Dinosaurs. This is an indoor ride that lasts about seven minutes and covers about 240 million years. You travel back into prehistoric times to meet such creatures as *Apatosaurus, Triceratops,* and *Tyrannosaurus rex.* The 21 animated models (which include some 13 dinosaurs) are skillfully designed and move in a chillingly lifelike manner. Special effects include crackling fires and bubbling tar pits. You'll hear dinosaur sounds and feel the heat from an erupting volcano and the chill of an Ice Age winter. The creators of the ride paid great attention to detail, so the experience is not only entertaining but educational.

The admission fee to enter the park includes the Kingdom of the Dinosaurs ride as well as many other rides and shows. Children under the age of two are admitted free. The park is open from 10:00 A.M. to 6:00 P.M. Monday through Friday, and later on Saturdays and Sundays. For more information call (714) 220-5200.

. . . and More

In the appendix you will find the addresses of the attractions described in this chapter as well as a list of other museums and parks in a state-by-state listing. Whether you and your child plan to visit the dinosaur's lair for a few hours or a few days, you're bound to find something wonderful within reach.

9

Finding Fossils

Although he is *greatly* exaggerated, in one aspect fictional archaeologist Indiana Jones represents an authentic view of science. The great body of human knowledge has not been collected solely in laboratories. Much of science is a "contact sport." Even as you read this book, botanists are trekking through remote jungles, zoologists are observing wild and exotic animals, meteorologists are braving the frigid Antarctic ice in search of clues to Earth's weather patterns, marine biologists are exploring the beauty and dangers of tropical reefs, and, all over the world, paleontologists are hunting for new clues to our planet's distant past. Science is an adventure, and a great way to express this to your youngster is to take part and experience the thrill of discovery.

Dinosaur remains have been found on every continent. However, even though sites in North America, particularly the American West, have yielded such creatures as *Apatosaurus, Stegosaurus,* and *Tyrannosaurus rex,* fossils of dinosaurs and other vertebrates are rare. Fortunately, fossils of invertebrates are comparatively common. You probably live within a day's drive of a site where, with a little planning and effort, your child can discover the remains of ancient plants or small sea creatures millions of years old. It isn't difficult to turn a day at the beach, a hike in the mountains, or a lakeside picnic into a fossil-hunting expedition (perhaps to unearth a specimen to add to the home museum). Hunting for fossils is an excellent way to learn patience (and persistence), to improve observational skills, and to simply enjoy nature. Even if your child doesn't find a fossil on the first outing, he or she need not go home empty-handed. An interesting example of sedimentary rock can make a fine addition to your child's collection.

The hunt will be of greater benefit and a lot more fun if you involve your youngster every step of the way. You may want to begin by sending away for an "official" dinosaur-hunting license from Dinah the dinosaur. It is not a permit to search for fossils, but rather a free, tongue-in-cheek hunting license that allows your child to capture a limited number of living dinosaurs should he or she happen across any. (It is good for four dinosaurs and four pteradactyls per person.) To obtain this special permit in your child's name, write to DINAH, Utah Field House, 235 East Main, Vernal, UT 84078. Include a legal-size, stamped, self-addressed envelope with your request.

READING ROCKS

The first step in planning your fossil expedition is deciding where to look. It's helpful to have a little background knowledge about the nature of rocks. Of the three types of rocks (categorized by the method of their formation), only one is likely to contain fossils. Earth's crust is for the most part composed of igneous ("fiery") rock, such as granite and basalt. It forms from molten material beneath the crust that flows to or near the surface, where it cools and eventually hardens. The odds of finding fossils in such material are virtually nil, because plant or animal remains would be destroyed during the formation process.

Metamorphic is from the Greek word meaning "changed." Metamorphic rock is material that has been changed from one form to another due to great heat, pressure, or chemical alteration. Marble (formed from limestone or dolomite) is an example. Even if fossils existed in the original material, it isn't likely that they would survive the transformation process.

Your best bet for finding fossils is in sedimentary rock. All rocks, no matter what their origin, are eventually worn down and eroded by the action of wind, water, changes in temperature, chemical action, and so forth to form sediments such as sand, silt, and mud. Following millions of years under pressure, such materials may form layers of new rock. For example, fine-grained mud and clay may become shale, and grains of sand may produce sandstone. Calcium carbonate, mostly from prehistoric corals and the shells of ancient sea animals, is the basis for limestone. The nature of sedimentary rock offers the best opportunity for fossilization. Although there is no guarantee that you will discover fossils, out-crops (areas that are exposed to the surface rather than covered by soil or vegetation) of sedimentary rock are where you should focus your attention.

> ***With your child:*** If you wanted to buy a pair of shoes, you would go to a store, but not all stores are the same. You wouldn't find shoes in a hardware store or a bookstore. Likewise, fossils are usually found in rocks, but not all rocks are the same. Here's help in explaining to your youngster which rocks might contain fossils.
>
> Some kinds of rock were once fiery, hot material that cooled and hardened. These are called igneous rocks. Other kinds of rock form when great heat and pressure changes them into a completely new material. These are called metamorphic rocks. Sedimentary rocks form from little bits of material such as sand and mud, called sedi-ment. Over millions of years, this material builds up, and the weight of all the sediment above causes the sediment at the bottom to cement together and form rock. Ask your youngster, "Of these three kinds of rock, in which type do you think you might find fossils? Why?"

Identifying Sedimentary Rocks

How can you recognize sedimentary rock? A visit to a lapidary or rock shop for a firsthand look is ideal. Toy stores often carry starter kits for young rock collectors. Begin with samples of three main "target rocks"—limestone, sandstone, and shale. If you can't find samples or a knowledgeable rock hound to take along on your expedition all is not lost. There are many handbooks available that can give you a good idea of what to look for. Here are a couple of helpful tips.

Sandstone, which may be found in a variety of colors including gray, tan, and red, is simple to recognize by its grainy texture. Through a small hand lens you can easily see individual grains.

Shale is dark in color, usually black, reddish, or gray-green. It is extremely fine-grained and will probably feel slightly slippery when wet. Shale wears away quickly. You're not likely to find outcrops of shale but you may find it a little below the surface between outcrops of sandstone.

Road cuts are a good place to search for this rock. Shale is an excellent source for unbroken fossils of sea creatures such as snail shells, clam shells, and, if you're lucky, the remains of trilobites.

Limestone is a fine-grained, whitish to light gray rock. The next time you go rock hunting, carry a small eyedropper bottle filled with vinegar. If you come across rock that you suspect is limestone, put a drop or two of vinegar on it. Calcium carbonate in the limestone will react with the vinegar, causing the liquid to fizz slightly.

Where the Rock Ends and Fossil Begins

Although you may be conducting your exploration hundreds of miles from the nearest water, the fossils you find are likely to be the remains of small, shelled sea creatures, many of which look much like animals living in the sea today. As you search, keep in mind the characteristic curves, swirls, and grooves of modern shells. Look for patterns, no matter how subtle, that seem unlike the surrounding rock. Fossilized plants also have their own distinctive patterns. There are usually slight color differences between a fossil and the rock that houses it. This may seem difficult to see at first, but don't give up. For some reason, kids seem to catch on quickly. Perhaps it is because they are natural observers. Don't be surprised if your youngster is the first to find a trophy!

> *Ask your child:* Millions of years ago, in parts of North America, the sea covered much of what is now dry land. Many of the rocky areas where scientists search for fossils formed underwater. What sort of creatures do you think we might find? What shapes and patterns do you think we should look for to detect such fossils?
> The fossils will probably be those of sea creatures with curved shell-like shapes.

Making plans

Appendix 2 contains several books that list possible fossil-hunting sites. There are other ways to find such sites, too. A member of the geology department at a local university or a nearby museum may be able to make a recommendation. The office of your state geological survey can help. They might have geological maps of your area that are available for a fee. Don't forget to try the rock shop. The owner or manager might know of a local geology club whose members can help you to get started.

If none of these sources turns up a suitable site, you may want to strike out on your own. Some good places to look are along beaches, streambeds, cliff faces, or gullies cut by running water. Cuts made for the passage of roads or train tracks sometimes expose fertile hunting grounds, as do construction sites.

The Rules of the Hunt

Following is a list of suggestions that will help make your adventure a pleasant experience. Review them with your youngster and discuss why each is important.

- Fossil-hunting is teamwork. Never hunt alone.

- Always ask permission from the owner before you enter or cross private property.

- If you are searching private land with permission, leave any gates in the same position you found them. Take your litter or trash with you.

- On public land find out if there are regulations that prohibit or restrict fossil collection. On most government land (such as that owned by the department of land management) you won't need a permit, but this isn't universal. Avoid any problems by checking with state or local agencies before you begin. All national parks restrict collecting unless special permission is given.

- Plan your outing in advance. Sketch out a route on a map of the area and stick close to it. Be sure that a friend or neighbor at home knows where you are going. It's also important to set a limit to the length of time you will search. Leave plenty of time to get back to your car or your camp before dark.

- Think safety! Wear gloves when moving small rocks that might be hiding places for insects, scorpions, snakes, or other animals. Use a stick to move the rock, or reach across with your gloved hand and lift the far edge of the rock slowly and carefully toward you. If there is an animal underneath, this will give it a chance to escape without giving it a clear shot at you. Most wild animals will retreat when faced by a human, but they will defend themselves if they are frightened or trapped.

- If you are collecting near a roadside or an area where you may come in contact with vehicles of any sort, keep well away from traffic. Stay out in the open where you can be easily seen.

- When scanning a spot at the base of a cliff, keep an eye out for loose rocks, and don't venture into caves. If you plan to investigate a slope or hillside, work from the bottom up and be careful not to dislodge material onto someone searching below.

- Be a courteous collector. Half of the fun is in the quest itself. There is no need to take everything you find. A specimen or two from each locale is a reasonable prize. Until you are comfortable with your fossil-hunting skills, it's best to search through rocks and gravel on the surface, but if you do dig a little, refill the holes when you are finished. Leave extensive digging to professionals.

What You'll Need:

Once you have selected a site, work with your child to choose the items you will take along on your adventure. Your fossil-hunting field kit will vary depending on the weather and the length of your expedition. Here is a checklist of tools you will need, along with a few other things that might come in handy. Take no more than you and your child can comfortably carry in a lightweight sack or backpack.

A geologist's hammer (available at a rock shop)
One or two cold steel chisels
One or two small brushes
A sieve or a small piece of wire screen
A tape measure
Plastic bags to hold specimens
Tissue or newspaper to wrap specimens
A notebook, a pencil, and a felt-tip pen
Lightweight safety goggles
Sturdy gloves
A map
Insect repellent
Sunscreen
A lightweight water canteen
Snacks
A small first-aid kit
A camera
A fossil identification guide

When the day of the hunt arrives, you and your child should wear comfortable clothing suitable for the weather, sturdy shoes, and a hat or cap to shield your eyes from the sun.

Finding Fossils

One important rule of science is to keep complete and accurate records. Before you begin your trek, help your child prepare a field notebook. The first entry should include location, time, date, and any observations about the area. Then keep the notebook handy for further notes. The keys to finding fossils are patience and a systematic search. Once again, planning is important. Map out a small area where you and your child will work together as a team. Search that area slowly and carefully before moving on to the next.

Broken material, called talus, at the base of an outcrop is a good source for small specimens that are already free of the parent rock, but you may find your treasure sealed in a chunk far too large to move. This is where that hammer and chisel come in handy. But wait—before you strike the first blow, document everything as carefully as possible. If you've brought a camera, take it out. Have your youngster assign an identification number to the fossil and write it on a piece of paper. Hold the paper next to the specimen and photograph it in place. If you don't have a camera, do a detailed sketch.

To remove the fossil, break away enough rock to make your find manageable. (Always point the chisel away from the specimen, and don't forget to wear your safety goggles.) Leave a wide margin of safety around the fossil to avoid any damage. You can do the finer work at home. With a felt-tip pen, write the identification number in an inconspicuous place on the fossil, then wrap your find carefully in newspaper or tissue. Be sure to record in the field notebook any important information about the position of the fossil, and the nature of the rock, and its surroundings.

Finding More Than You Bargained for

Suppose that while you are looking for prehistoric seashells you come across what looks like a *Tyrannosaurus* skull. After you recover from the shock, resist the desire to probe further. Photograph or sketch the find, note its location on the map, and jot down any details that will help the experts identify the fossil and find it again. Then cover it up. Send the data to a local university or museum. If the discovery is indeed an important one, it's best handled by professionals so that it won't be damaged, and so that vital information in the surrounding area is not lost.

Your youngster might like to know that children have been responsible for many outstanding fossil finds. In 1802, 12-year-old Pliny Moody was helping to plow a field on a Massachusetts farm. He turned up more than rich soil. In fact, he uncovered gigantic birdlike tracks that appeared to be etched in stone. No one had even heard of dinosaurs yet, so most people thought the tracks had been made by huge birds. Many years later, the remarkable footprints were correctly identified as those of a dinosaur.

Young Mary Anning often accompanied her father on fossil-hunting trips in England. Mary was just 12 in 1810 when she uncovered the world's first ichthyosaur remains to be recognized as a new species. As she grew older, she went onto discover other firsts, including the first plesiosaur remains and, in 1828, the first pterosaur remains found in Britain.

For 10-year-old Colin McEwan of Virgina, a school field trip turned into an event he will always remember. While climbing around in a pile of dirt left behind by workmen, he noticed a most unusual rock—one that proved to be the vertebrae of a plesiosaur! Because of this alert young man, this important fossil now rests in the Smithsonian.

Preparing the Display

Even if the fossils you locate are of a more common variety, the adventure is not over once your discovery is safely wrapped, labeled, and tucked away. Set aside a convenient area at home where you can work with your child to clean and prepare your find for display. You can divide the responsibilities depending on your youngster's age. For example, you can remove any outer rock while your child brushes away loose grains. Create a holder for the fossil by filling a small sack with sand. The sack can be molded to safely cradle the fossil in different positions as you work. Carefully chip away any surface rock a little bit at a time, always pointing the tool away from the fossil. Wash the finished product carefully in mild, soapy water and dry it completely with a soft cloth. Repair any cracks or breaks in the specimen with white glue.

Now you are ready to catalog the fossil. First, record the identification number of the specimen in a collection record book or on a 3 × 5 card. Have your child transfer any important information about the fossil to this record. He or she should include the location where the object was found, the date of collection, the type of rock in which the specimen occurred, the name of the collector, catalog numbers of any other objects discovered in the same area, and the type of fossil it is. Once the record is complete, the exhibit is ready for display. Larger objects may need a special place on a suitable shelf. An empty egg carton with a little cotton padding in the bottom of each section is excellent for presenting small specimens for family and friends to admire.

From beginning to end, the fossil-hunting experience is a delightful way to help your child better understand the careful study and planning that is critical to good science. Time in the field will reinforce a healthy respect for nature and encourage his or her curiosity about the wonderful mysteries our planet holds.

10

Let's Have a Party

Now that you are a dinosaur aesthete, why not make these marvelous beasts the theme of your youngster's next birthday celebration? This chapter offers a "prehistoric party" plan, including suggestions for decorations, party hats, and edible treats, as well as a selection of games and riddles. Be creative and think of your own ideas, too!

There is no shortage of materials available to help you set the stage. No matter where you live, you are sure to find dinosaur posters, models, and books in local toy stores. Such stores are treasure troves of plastic models, pencils, erasers, coloring books, balloons, and other items with a dinosaur motif that make perfect party favors and game prizes. At the candy store you can buy jellybeans to use as pebbles, licorice whips for vines, and candy corn that can double as mock dinosaur teeth.

To carry home their goodies, provide each party guest with a paper sack that has his or her name written on it in "dinosaur style" (*Andreasaurus, Kristinadon,* or *Andrewceratops,* for example). Keep the sacks in one spot so that the youngsters have a safe place to store their prizes and party favors during the festivities.

Creating the Scene

Lush ferns flourished during the Mesozoic Era, and such plants could certainly dress up a party table, but there is no need to rush to the nearest nursery. By following the directions below, you and your child can make lacy ferns of construction paper. Add vines made of colored cord and turn the party area into a Jurassic jungle.

Materials:

12-inch × 9-inch sheets of green construction paper (2-3 sheets for each fern)
A pencil
Tape
Toothpicks
Scissors
Modeling clay
Thin, flexible wire

Instructions:

1. Here's how to make one fern. Fold two sheets of construction paper into thirds the long way, then cut along the folds. You should have six three-inch-wide strips.
2. Fold each strip in half. Draw a wavy line (as shown in the illustration) along the open edge of each strip, then cut along the line and unfold the paper.
3. Repeat this with each strip and you will have six long fern leaves.

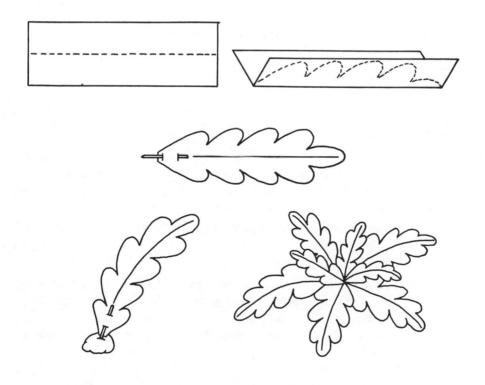

4. For four smaller leaves, fold one sheet of construction paper into quarters the short way. Cut along the folds and follow step 2 above.
5. Once the leaves are complete, use the scissors to poke two small holes in the stem ends one inch apart. Take each leaf and thread a toothpick in one hole and out the other.
6. Roll a ball of modeling clay about one inch in diameter. Flatten the clay at the base. Holding each leaf by its toothpick, insert each toothpick into the clay until the fern is complete. (If you wish to position the leaves in a particular way, cut a length of wire and tape it to one side of each leaf, then shape the wire as you like.) You can vary the size of the paper plants by adding more leaves or cutting shorter leaves.

Crown-toppers

Instead of party hats, why not cap each young guest with paper crest, frills, and horns? In fact, with a little help the youngsters may enjoy constructing their own headgear or masks.

Materials:
Construction paper (at least three large sheets per guest)
Pencils
Tape
Scissors

To make a crest:
1. Cut a two-inch-wide strip lengthwise from a sheet of construction paper, then fold the strip in half. Tape the ends together to form a band that will fit snugly around the child's head. (You may have to add paper at one end to make the band fit properly).
2. Cut a second strip in the same manner. Place this strip across the top of the child's head and tape one end to the front and the other end to the back of the headband.
3. Fold another piece of construction paper in half. With the fold at the top, use a pencil to draw a crest such as that of a *Lambeosaurus* or *Corythosaurus.* Curve the base of the crest so it will fit along the top strip on the headband. Draw three or four tabs at the base of the crest.

4. Carefully cut out the crest with the tabs. Center in on the top strip of the headband and draw lines where the tabs and headband meet.

5. Cut slots where you made the marks. Push each pair of tabs through the slots, fold the tabs back, and tape them down so that the crest stands securely.

To make a frill and horns:

1. Follow steps 1 and 2 above.

2. Fold another piece of construction paper in half. Draw two long, curved horns with tabs at the base and cut them out. Mark and cut two slots in the front of the headband so that the horns will be positioned over the child's eyes. Push the tabs through the slots and secure them underneath with tape.

3. To make the frill, draw a deep crescent shape on another piece of construction paper. Make sure you draw four tabs along the inner curve. Along the outer curve draw spikes or knobs if you like. Now cut out the frill. Hold the frill to the back of the headband, marking where the tabs and headband meet.

4. Cut slots for each tab, then push the tabs through and tape them in place. The frill should rest along the back of the child's neck.

Marvelous Masks

Materials:

Paper grocery bags
Lightweight paper plates
Felt-tip markers
Glue
Scissors
Tape
Scrap material such as yarn, fabric, dried pasta, paper-towel tubes

Instructions:

1. Prepare an area where the children can work and easily share materials while making their masks.

2. Give each youngster a grocery bag. Help him or her trim the bag to a size that will comfortably fit over his or her head. Help cut out eye holes in each bag.

3. Let the youngsters design and decorate their masks from the scrap materials you have provided. There's plenty of room here for creativity. A paper plate cut in half could be used as a crest or a duckbill's snout. Cardboard paper rolls makes impressive horns, dried macaroni might serve as long, curved teeth, and a swatch of fabric could be a lolling tongue.

Let the Games Begin!

Before long you will find yourself in the midst of a most unusual and probably energetic herd of dinosaurs. The games that follow will help keep them happily and safely entertained. Most are suitable for playing indoors and can be adjusted to entertain youngsters from 6 to 12 years old. The games that need pre-party preparation are marked with an asterisk.

*Find Your Twin

This activity is a great icebreaker for a large group.

Materials:

Name tags
Safety pins

Instructions:

1. Before the party, choose the names of a number of dinosaurs. The number you need depends on your guest list. Print each name on two separate name tags so that you have a pair of tags with the same name. The tags should be large enough that the name is easy to read. Make enough name tags so that you have one for each party guest.
2. When the children are ready to play the game, pin one tag to each child's back. Don't let the youngster see the name on the paper.
3. When everyone has a tag, tell the children to try to find their "twins." Each child may not look at his or her own tag but may ask questions of other players that can be answered with a "yes" or "no," for example, "Am I a four-legged dinosaur?" or "Am I a meat-eater?"
4. The game is over when the last pair is matched.

Cross the River

To play this game the children should have a little knowledge of dinosaurs.

Materials:

20 pieces of light cardboard or construction paper to use as stepping stones
A pair of dice

Instructions:

1. Arrange the paper in two rows across the floor. Each piece represents a stepping stone across a raging river.
2. Divide the group into two teams, the sauropods and theropods. Have a member of the sauropods stand at the beginning of one row and a member of the theropods at the beginning of the other row. The object is for each team to move its representative across the river one step at a time by answering questions correctly. The first team to reach the opposite "bank" wins. (See the following section for examples of questions to ask.)
3. To avoid having the players yell out the answers, have a member from each team roll one die. The child with the highest number gets to try to answer the first question. He or she can ask team members for help before giving an answer. If the answer is correct, that team's representative moves forward one stepping stone. If the answer is incorrect, the other team gets a chance to answer the same question. If their answer is correct, their representative moves forward.
4. The die is passed to the next member of each team and the game continues until there is a winner.

Sample Questions:

Use these questions to play Cross the River, or make up your own. Adjust the difficulty according to the age range of the youngsters.

1. What is the name of the era when the dinosaurs lived?
   The Mesozoic Era.

2. The snout of duckbilled dinosaurs resembled the beak of what modern animal?
   A duck.

3. Which was not a dinosaur: *Apatosaurus, Iguanodon,* or *Pteranodon*?
   Pteranodon.

4. Which dinosaur has a name that means "tyrant lizard"?
   Tyrannosaurus rex.

5. What strange feature did *Stegosaurus* have on its back?
   A row of bony plates.

6. Which dinosaur was biggest: *Coelophysis, Deinonychus,* or *Apatosaurus*?
   Apatosaurus.

7. How many horns did *Triceratops* have on its face?
   Three.

8. What did *Iguanodon* eat?
   Plants.

9. How many periods make up the Mesozoic Era?
   Three.

10. Which dinosaur was smallest: *Saltopus, Ultrasaurus,* or *Stegosaurus*?
    Saltopus.

11. Were there any flying dinosaurs?
    No.

12. Which dinosaur was a meat-eater: *Triceratops, Maiasaura,* or *Allosaurus*?
    Allosaurus.

13. Are there any dinosaurs alive today?
    No.

14. What sort of skin did dinosaurs have?
    Scaly.

15. Which modern animals are most closely related to the dinosaurs?
    Birds.

16. What are dinosaur remains called?
    Fossils.

17. How long ago did the dinosaurs disappear?
    65 million years ago.

18. Name a large modern animal that has changed very little since the time of the dinosaurs.
    The crocodile.

19. On which continents have dinosaur fossils been found?
    All the continents.

20. Spell "dinosaur."

Caught in the Act

Materials:

A beanbag or large raw potato
A whistle
A blindfold

Instructions:

1. Have the guests form a ring around your child, who is blindfolded and holding the whistle. The bean bag or potato represents a dinosaur egg. The egg is passed from one player to the next around the circle. The object of the game is not to be caught with the egg when your child blows the whistle.
2. When the whistle is blown, the player holding the egg (or in case the egg is dropped, the last player to have held it) must leave the circle. Everyone else remains in exactly the same place.
3. As each child is eliminated and gaps appear in the circle, it becomes more difficult to pass the egg. The last player left in the circle is the winner.

*True or False

Materials:

3 × 5 cards
A shoe box
A pencil

Instructions:

1. You will need enough 3 × 5 cards so that each guest will have one. Before the party, separate the cards into two equal stacks. Pick one stack and write the name of a different, obscure dinosaur and several true facts about the animal (the more outrageous the better) on each card in the stack. On each card in the second stack, write the name of a different make-believe dinosaur along with phony, madeup "facts" about that animal on each card. Place the cards face down in the shoe box.

2. Each child takes a turn and picks a card. The child reads the information on the card to the group as convincingly as possible.

3. Each member of the group decides whether the dinosaur is real or fake, and a vote is taken. The object is to fool as many people as possible. Keep score by counting the number of "true" and "false" votes, and note whether each vote is correct or not. The player that gets the highest number of "wrong" votes wins.

Pass It On

Materials:

Two ping pong balls

Empty cardboard rolls from gift wrap (cut into thirds), paper towels, or bathroom tissue (if you can't collect enough of these you can make rolls by taping sheets of construction paper into cylinders).

Instructions:

1. Divide the guests into two groups and have them form two lines.

2. Give each child a cardboard tube or construction-paper cylinder.

3. The ping-pong balls will serve as dinosaur eggs. Beginning with the first child in line, place a dinosaur egg into the tube he or she is holding. Each group must "lay" its egg by passing the ball from tube to tube until it reaches the end of the line. If the egg is dropped before reaching the end, the group must start over from the beginning of the line.

4. The first team to transport its egg safely to the end of the line wins.

**Treasure Hunt*

This game is loads of fun because everyone is on his or her own adventure. It is also a way to be sure that every guest wins at least one prize.

Materials:

Small prizes or "treasures" (one for each guest)
A treasure map for every prize

Instructions:

1. Before the party, number each prize in some manner and hide all of them. Make a treasure map for each hiding place. At the top of the map, write the number that corresponds to the number on the prize, then write several clues that will help direct the child in his or her search. Each clue should bring the youngster closer to the treasure.
2. The hunt begins when each child is given a map and assigned a starting place according to the instructions. The rest is up to them.
3. If a child finds a treasure that has a number different to the one on his or her map, the prize should be left in place so that the proper map holder can find it. When the search is over, everyone will be a winner!

Thief

Materials:

A bone (any small object can be used as the bone)

Instructions:

1. One child is chosen to be "It." This child is the scientist who has just unearthed a valuable fossil. He or she sits with eyes closed facing away from the rest of the children, who are pretending to be a pack of playful dogs. The bone is behind the "Scientist's" back.
2. Quietly point to one "dog" at a time. The child you select must leave his or her place and try to sneak up on the scientist and steal the bone. If the scientist suspects that someone is trying to take his fossil, he or she says, "Is that a dog come to steal my bone?"

3. If a player is actually holding the bone and has not yet returned to his or her original place, that player must answer with a bark. If the scientist can identify the "dog" by name, the two children exchange places and the "dog" becomes the "scientist." If the scientist incorrectly identifies the dog, the player must put the bone back and return to the group.

4. If a player succeeds in stealing the bone and returning to his or her original position without being caught, all of the children call out "Doctor, Doctor, who has your bone?" The scientist may turn around and look at the group and try to guess the culprit. If he or she is correct, the two children exchange places. If the dog fools the scientist, he or she gets a point.

5. Set a time limit for the game. The player with the most points at the end of the game is the winner.

Mixed-up Dinosaurs

This quiet activity can be enjoyed around a large table.

Materials:

Pencils or crayons

Enough sheets of drawing paper so that every guest has one. Before the party, fold each sheet of paper into thirds, make sharp creases, then unfold.

Instructions:

1. Have the children sit or stand around a table. Give each youngster one sheet of paper and something to draw with and ask them to draw the *head* of a dinosaur on the top third of the paper. Only the lines of the neck should extend slightly below the crease.

2. When everyone is finished, have each guest fold the section with the head back so that it cannot be seen, then pass the paper to the artist on his or her right. Now ask the children to draw the *body* of the dinosaur on the middle third of the paper. The lines should continue just a little past the lower crease.

3. When everyone is finished, have each child fold the second section back so that only the last third can be seen. Each drawing is passed to the right, and each child now draws legs in the third section.

4. Collect all of the drawings and unfold them one at a time, showing the children the hilarious results of their work.

With a few twists, many games that are old favorites can be adapted to the dinosaur theme.

*Charades

Materials:

3 × 5 cards
A shoe box

Instructions:

1. Write the names of well-known dinosaurs and four simple facts about each animal on 3 × 5 cards. Put a different dinosaur on each card. Make enough cards so that every guest will have one, then place the cards face down in a shoe box.
2. Divide the group into two teams. The first "contestant" must draw a card and then wordlessly act out the dinosaur to his or her team.
3. If no one on the team can guess the dinosaur, the child can give them a hint by reading aloud one of the facts written on the card while continuing to act the part.
4. If the team guesses without needing a hint, they score five points. One point is deducted for each hint given. If they guess only after receiving all four hints, then the team gets only one point.
5. When all of the players have had a chance, add up the score to see which team wins.

*Pin the Tail on the Dinosaur

Materials:

A dinosaur poster
Paper
Tape
A blindfold

Instructions:

1. Before the party, draw a number of tails (one for each party guest) for the dinosaur. Write a guest's name on each tail and attach a piece of tape at one end so that a sticky portion is left exposed.

2. Each child in turn is blindfolded and directed toward the poster to attach a paper tail to the dinosaur precisely over the tail in the picture. The child who comes closest to the right area wins.

Dinosaur Dash

This relay race has a prehistoric turn: all the players must "run" on all fours like giant dinosaurs.

Materials:

None

Instructions:

1. Begin with two teams. Divide each team into two groups (group A and group B) that will form lines at opposite ends of the room. (For a large party this game is better played in the backyard or a park. In this case you can widen the area to be covered in the race.)

2. When you say "go," the first child in group A for each team must run on all fours to the other side and tap the first runner in group B, who then runs to the opposite side. The race continues back and forth until every runner on one team has crossed the finish line. That team is the winner.

*Scavenger Hunt

Finally, what better activity for a dinosaur party than a search for prehistoric remains? Of course, unless most of your neighbors are paleontologists, you will have to use a little imagination when making up the object lists.

Materials:

Two lists of objects

Instructions:

1. Set up two teams of youngsters. Each team should be accompanied by one or two adults. Provide the adults with a list of 20 or 30 items to be scavenged.
2. Set a limit of one hour. During that time, the two teams will take off in opposite directions and try to locate as many items on the list as possible. The team that comes closest to completing the challenge wins.

Here are a few suggestions to get your list started:

A dinosaur egg (a hen's egg will do—be careful not to break it!)

A dinosaur claw (a false fingernail)

A dinosaur bone (any bone, even a dog toy)

A shell

Four white pebbles

A fern leaf

A picture or model of a dinosaur

Dinosaur scales (perhaps fish scales or sequins)

DELECTABLE DINOSAURS

Your guests are certain to work up an appetite. Even a hungry tyrannosaur can be appeased with these goodies. Your child can easily prepare these simple sugar cookies for the party. An asterisk marks steps that will need *your* close attention.

INGREDIENTS

$^1\!/_2$ *cup butter*

$^1\!/_2$ *cup sugar*

$2^1\!/_2$ *cups white flour*

2 *teaspoons baking powder*

$^1\!/_2$ *teaspoon cinnamon*

$^1\!/_2$ *teaspoon salt*

1 *teaspoon vanilla*

2 *eggs*

2 *heaping teaspoons sugar*

Green food coloring

1.* Many specialty shops devoted to cooking and baking supplies now carry dinosaur-shaped cookie cutters. However, you can make forms by cutting pictures of two or three different dinosaurs from a coloring book (the basic shapes in such books are ideal, but if you want to keep it extremely simple, you only need to create a pattern for a large dinosaur footprint). Trace the shapes onto a piece of heavy cardboard and cut out the forms.

2.* Preheat your oven to 375 degrees and grease a cookie sheet.

3. Prepare the cookie dough by combining the butter with ½ cup sugar until the mixture is soft and creamy.

4. Mix in the flour, baking powder, cinnamon, salt, eggs, and vanilla. If you like, add three or four drops of green food coloring. Chill the prepared dough for about three hours.

5. On a lightly floured board, roll the dough until it is about ¼" thick.

6.* If you are using cardboard patterns to make the dinosaur shapes, dust each pattern with flour. Place each pattern on the dough as a guide and cut around it with a knife. If the patterns are simple, this will not be too time-consuming.

7. Place the cookies on the greased cookie sheet, leaving a little space between each one.

8.* Bake for about 20 minutes or until lightly browned.

9. While the treats are in the oven, combine two heaping tablespoons of sugar with two drops of green food coloring. Mix well.

10.* When the cookies are ready, remove them from the oven, sprinkle each with the special sugar mixture, and allow them to cool. Makes about three dozen cookies.

CRETACEOUS CUPCAKE CONES

This treat is simple, but its prehistoric patterns make it extra special.

INGREDIENTS

One box of chocolate cake mix

Sugar cones (the kind used for ice cream)

Powdered sugar

1. These unusual cupcakes are topped with a two-inch stenciled dinosaur design. You can make a small stencil by cutting a simple shape such as a footprint from light cardboard. Discard the center and keep the outline only.

2. Prepared the cake mix according to the directions on the package. Fill as many sugar cones as you can to the halfway point. Place the cones upright on a baking sheet.

3. Bake according to the package directions.

4. When the cupcakes are completed, remove from the oven and allow them to cool slightly. Next, place your stencil over the top of each cupcake and dust each with powdered sugar. When you remove the stencil, you'll have a nice white picture on each cupcake!

MESOZOIC METEORITES

These bite-sized goodies can be made several days ahead of time and stored in a container with a tight-fitting lid.

INGREDIENTS

½ cup butter

2 tablespoons sugar

1 teaspoon vanilla

1 cup flour

¾ cup finely ground pecans (use a food processor for this)

Powdered sugar

1. Preheat the oven to 300 degrees.

2. Mix all the ingredients (except the powdered sugar) into a firm but slightly sticky batter.

3. With your hands, roll about one teaspoonful of batter at a time into balls and place them on a greased cookie sheet. Bake for 40 to 45 minutes.

4. Fill a small bowl with powdered sugar. When the cookies are done, allow them to cool to room temperature, then roll each one in powdered sugar until it is lightly coated.

STRATIFIED SWEETS

This dish is easy to prepare, but make sure you allow enough preparation time.

INGREDIENTS

One package of graham cracker crust mix

One box each of lime gelatin, lemon gelatin, and strawberry gelatin

1 cup crushed walnuts

1 cup sliced bananas

1 cup sliced strawberries
Whipped cream

1. Prepare the graham cracker crust mix and use it to line an 8 × 12 × 2 glass pan.

2. Prepare the lime gelatin following the package directions and allow it to cool to room temperature. Then pour the gelatin into the prepared pan. Chill several hours until firm.

3. Now prepare the lemon gelatin. Refrigerate it until slightly firm, then mix in the sliced bananas and pour it over the lime gelatin. Return the pan to the refrigerator for several hours.

4. Repeat with the strawberry gelatin, mixing in the strawberries and crushed walnuts.

5. Before serving, top the dessert with a layer of whipped cream. Cut into squares and serve.

A STEGOSAUR THAT TAKES THE CAKE

Of course, no birthday celebration is complete without the cake. This *Stegosaurus* pattern is designed to be cut from a 14-inch × 11-inch sheet cake. Once the pieces are properly arranged on a platter and iced, add chocolate chip cookie halves for dinosaur plates, and gum drops for eyes. This dinosaur display is likely to be the main attraction at your party!

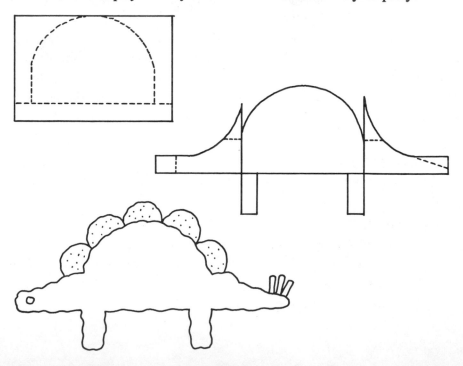

11

What's In a Name?

About 150 years ago, as evidence mounted that certain fossils were indeed the remains of a new suborder of animals, it became apparent that the creatures needed a name. In 1841, British comparative anatomist Dr. Richard Owen combined the Greek word *deinos,* meaning "terrible," with *sauros,* meaning "lizard," and christened the beasts "Dinosauria." In spite of the fact that the animals weren't lizards (whether or not they were truly "terrible" is a matter of opinion), the name has endured.

The word *dinosaur* seems reasonable enough. So why are the family, genus, and species names such tongue twisters? Why not simple names such as those for modern birds like *robin, mockingbird,* and *crow*?

Actually, our familiar feathered friends also have names that defy verbalization. To a scientist, the mockingbird is *Mimus polyglottos,* and the common crow is known as *Corvus brachyrhynchos.* The long scientific names are a sort of international language that helps avoid confusion when identifying a plant or animal. It is not uncommon for two unrelated birds in widely separated countries to share a common name. For example, to an American, the charming, red-breasted *Turdus migratorius* is a "robin," but to the British a "robin" is a similar but unrelated bird (*Erithacus rubecula*). Conversely, *Plautus alle* is a "little auk" in Great Britain, while in North America the very same bird is commonly known as a dovkie. Obviously, there is plenty of room for misunderstanding in this system, so all plants and animals have a universally recognized scientific name derived from Greek or Latin.

The practice began when eighteenth-century Swedish botanist Carl von Linné (who later Latinized his own name to Carolus Linnaeus) created a catalog of all living things. He assigned each organism a generic or *genus* name and a specific or *species* name according to the organism's physical characteristics. He developed the larger classifications of family, order, and so forth later. Known as binomial nomenclature, this practice was widely used and accepted by the time the dinosaurs were discovered. Since then dinosaur fossils have been unearthed on every continent and, regardless of geographical or political borders, scientists of every nationality confer each new animal with a name according to this system. The discoverer generally chooses a name that describes or incorporates one or more of three elements: a characteristic of the animal (*Stegosaurus,* or "plated lizard"); the place where the animal was found (*Saltasaurus,* for the Salta Province in Argentina); or the name of a person involved in the find (*Baryonyx walkeri,* or "Walker's strong claw").

Just hearing an animal's name can often give you a hint to the type of creature it was. For example, *tri* means "three" and *cerato* means "horned." Knowing this you can safely assume that *Triceratops* had three horns. Once you get used to the system, the names are no more difficult to remember than words like *rhododendron, vertebrate, hypodermic,* or *isometric.* Knowing the meaning of a few simple, commonly used Greek or Latin roots is the key. The root words listed below will give you a good start. Once you get the hang of it, you and your youngster can put some of these roots together to create new Greek or Latin names for pets and family. For example, if your dog has long, fluffy ears and a short tail, it could be a *Dasyotomicrourus.* Use your imagination!

PREFIX	LANGUAGE	PRONUNCIATION	MEANING
a-	G	AY	without
abricto-	G	uh-BRIK-toh	wide awake
aeto-	L	AY-toh	aged
alectro-	G	uh-LEK-troh	unmarried, alone
allo-	G	AL-oh	other
alti-	L	AL-tee	high
anato-	L	uh-NAT-oh	duck
aniso-	G	a-NEE-so	unequal
antarcto-	G	ant-ARK-to	southern
antro-	G	AN-tro	cavern
apato-	G	uh-PAT-uh	deceptive
aqua-	L	AH-kwah	water
archi-	G	AR-kee	primitive

aristo-	G	uh-RIST-oh	best
astro-	G	AS-troh	star
atro-	L	A-troh	black
auri-	L	OR-ee	ear
baro-	G	BARE-uh	heavy
brachio-	G	BRAYK-ee-oh	arm
brachy-	G	BRAK-ee	short
bronto-	G	BRON-tuh	thunder
camara-	G	KAM-uh-ruh	chamber
campto-	G	KAMP-toh	bent
cerato-	G	sayr-AT-oh	horned
coel-	L	SEEL	hollow
compso-	G	COMP-soh	elegant
cory-	G	KOR-ee	helmet
dasy-	G	DAZ-ee	hairy
di-	G	DY	two
dino-	G	DY-nuh	terrible
diplo-	G	DIP-luh	double
dryo-	G	DRY-uh	oak
ecto-	G	EK-toh	outside
elaphro-	G	ee-LAF-roh	lightweight
endo-	G	EN-doh	inside
erythro-	G	eh-REE-throh	red
frigo-	L	FREE-goh	cold
hetero-	G	HET-er-oh	different
hypsi-	G	HIP-see	high
kentro-	G	KEN-troh	spiked
lepto-	G	LEP-toh	weak
mani-	L	MAHN-ee	hand
megalo-	G	MEG-uh-loh	large
micro-	G	MI-kroh	small
mono-	G	MAHN-oh	one
nano-	G	NAN-oh	dwarf
naso-	L	NAY-zoh	nose
necto-	G	NEK-toh	swimming
neo-	G	NEE-oh	new
noto-	G	NOH-toh	back
octo-	G	OK-toh	eight
omni-	G	OM-nee	all
ophio-	G	O-fee-oh	serpent

ornitho-	G	OR-nith-oh	bird
osmo-	G	OZ-moh	smell
oto-	G	O-toh	ear
ovi-	L	O-vee	egg
pachy-	G	PAK-ee	thick
patri-	G	PAH-tree	father
penta-	G	PEN-tuh	five
phago-	G	FAY-joh	eating
platy-	G	PLAT-ee	wide, flat
plesio-	G	PLEE-zee-oh	near
poly-	G	PAHL-ee	many
proto-	G	PRO-toh	first
pseudo-	G	SOO-doh	false
ptero-	G	TAYR-oh	wing
retro-	L	REH-troh	backward
rhodo-	G	ROH-doh	red
salto-	L	SAL-toh	leaping
sapro-	G	SAP-roh	rotten
sarco-	G	SAR-koh	flesh
saur-	G	SORE	lizard
sclero-	G	SKLAYR-oh	hard
spheno-	G	SFEE-noh	wedge-shaped
stego-	G	STEG-uh	roofed, plated
tecno-	G	TEK-noh	child
tenui-	L	TEN-wee	thin
tetra-	G	TET-ruh	four
thero-	G	THAYR-uh	beast
titano-	G	ti-TAN-oh	gigantic
tri-	G	TRY	three
tyranno-	G	ty-RAN-oh	tyrant
ultra-	L	UL-tra	beyond
veloci-	L	vel-AH-see	swift
xeno-	G	ZEE-noh	strange

SUFFIX	LANGUAGE	PRONUNCIATION	MEANING
-cephalic	G	seh-FAL-ik	head
-dactyl	G	DAK-til	finger
-demus	G	DEE-mus	body
-docus	G	DO-kus	beam
-gnathus	G	NAY-thus	jaw

-ichthys	G	IK-this	fish
-ischian	G	ISS-kee-an	hip joint
-lestes	G	LESS-teez	robber
-lophus	G	LOW-fus	crested
-mimus	L	MY-mus	mimic
-nychus	G	NYK-us	claw
-odon	G	oh-DON	tooth
-pod	L	PAHD	foot
-pteryx	G	TAYR-iks	wing
-raptor	L	RAP-tor	thief
-saurus	G	SORE-us	lizard
-spinax	L	SPIN-ax	spine
-urus	G	UR-us	tail
-venator	G	VEN-uh-tor	hunter

Master these and you will not only be able to easily identify denizens of prehistory by name, you will actually be able to speak "dinosaur" with your child.

12

The Top 20:
Questions and Answers

Perhaps the single most important thing you can do to encourage her or his understanding of the natural world is invite your child to ask questions (and to assure them that there are no "dumb" questions). In his book *Teach Your Child Science,* Michael Shermer points out that science is not a matter of *what* to think, but *how* to think. He stresses the importance of objectivity, mental flexibility, the confidence to challenge the current wisdom, and the creativity to tackle a problem from several directions and develop viable solutions. In *Sleuthing Fossils,* geologist Dr. Alan Cvancara reminds us of the proverb: A human mind is like a parachute—it works best when open. The study of ancient life is an excellent example of these mental processes in action. What color were the dinosaurs? What sorts of sounds did they make? In the years that I have spent writing for children and visiting classrooms I have found that youngsters are eager to ask questions. For my own reference, I have put together a file of the questions that are most common. This file is the source of the "top 20" listed below.

QUESTIONS AND ANSWERS

Where does the name dinosaur *come from?*

During the early 1800s, dinosaur remains were first recognized as being those of a new order of animal. The creatures were thought to be huge and lizardlike. In 1841, comparative anatomist Dr. Richard Owen coined the word dinosaur from two Greek words, *deinos* and *sauros,* meaning "terrible lizard."

How do we know that dinosaurs really lived?

We know that dinosaurs lived and we learn when and how they lived by studying their fossilized remains.

Where did dinosaurs live?

Dinosaur fossils have been found on every continent. (Because the face of the Earth is always slowly changing, our modern land masses were positioned quite differently during the age of dinosaurs.) Dinosaurs lived in a variety of habitats from arid deserts to lush swamps. They were, however, land-dwellers. Although many other varieties of reptile sometimes swam in Mesozoic waters, there were no sea-going dinosaurs.

How many dinosaurs were there?

At the present time about 300 different genera of dinosaurs are known.

Which was the first dinosaur?

This is a difficult question to answer because we do not have (and may never have) an uninterrupted fossil record of life at the dawn of the Mesozoic Era. One very early dinosaur is *Herrerasaurus.* Its remains were discovered in rock that is between 225 and 230 million years old.

Were dinosaurs smart?

Based on brain size compared to body size alone, it appears that most dinosaurs were not as "smart" as modern birds and mammals. Scientists can get a fairly accurate estimate of the size of an animal's brain by making a cast of the inside of the skull. The brain of a 30-ton *Apatosaurus* was about the same size as that of a 50-pound dog. The brain of a two-ton *Stegosaurus* was very small, only the size of a golfball. On the other hand, theropods appear to have had relatively large brains. *Stenonychosaurus,* sometimes considered the most intelligent dinosaur, had a brain seven times the size of other archosaurs of similar body weight. Still, brain size is not the only measure of a capable and successful species. The dinosaurs survived for more than 140 million years on Earth, which is a record that, at this point, humans are not even close to matching.

How old could a dinosaur live to be?

As with modern animals, the lifespan of a dinosaur was probably dependent on its species. There is fossil evidence (growth rings in bones) that certain large dinosaurs reached ages of 120 years and older. Scientists also speculate that many species continued to grow throughout their lives.

Did dinosaurs talk to each other?

Dinosaurs did not "talk" to others in a human sense, but it's likely that they communicated. Some may have roared or squealed. Hollow-crested dinosaurs may have used their special headgear to amplify sound. Physical markings and patterns are also a form of visual communication that may have been important to dinosaurs.

What sounds did dinosaurs make?

No one can say for certain what sounds, if any, dinosaurs made. As with modern creatures, each species possibly had a distinctive call or perhaps several calls depending on the situation. During the Mesozoic Era, the air was probably filled with squeals, shrieks, whinnies, screeches, snorts, bellows, wails, and roars.

What color were the dinosaurs?

We can only guess what colors or markings dinosaurs displayed, but modern reptiles offer possible clues. Reptiles often exhibit colors or patterns that may attract mates, discourage enemies, or enable the creatures to blend with their surroundings. There is no reason to think that dinosaurs were any different. In fact, the mummified remains of one *Anatosaurus,* complete with patches of dried skin, showed signs of a speckled pattern.

How big were dinosaur eggs?

The size of dinosaur eggs varied depending on the species, but even the largest known were only about the size of a football. Jumbo eggs would have been impractical. The larger the egg, the thicker the shell would need to be. At some point, such an eggshell would be too thick for a hatchling to break through. Some scientists speculate that dinosaurs such as *Apatosaurus* gave birth to live young, but there is no physical evidence to support this.

How big were baby dinosaurs?

Fossil remains of hatchlings and juveniles are not available for every type of dinosaur, and, once again, the answer is different for each species. When it hatched, *Protoceratops* was about 12 inches long, or approximately the length of a small housecat. A fossil baby *Psittacosaurus* was discovered that was only 10 inches long. It seems that the young of certain species grew very quickly. A *Maiasaura* baby that was only 12 inches long at birth might reach a length of 10 feet in its first year.

Were baby dinosaurs cute?

There is evidence that the snouts of duckbilled dinosaurs were quite short at birth, giving the hatchlings an appearance that humans would probably describe as "cute." An adult *Corythosaurus* had a flat crest on its head that looked like half a dinner plate set on edge. In young corythosaurs, the crest was barely developed. In newborn horned dinosaurs such as *Chasmosaurus,* the impressive horns and neck frill were probably quite small.

Which was the largest dinosaur?

There were many huge dinosaurs, but the prize for the biggest probably goes to *Seismosaurus*. From the size of the bones, paleontologists have figured out that this sauropod was 120 to 140 feet long, and weighed well over 80 tons. *Tyrannosaurus* still holds the title of largest meat-eating dinosaur.

Were there any small dinosaurs?

Yes, there were many small dinosaurs. At about two feet long from nose to tail, *Saltopus* and *Compsognathus* were smaller than many house pets. *Deinonychus,* one of the fiercest Cretaceous predators, was no taller or heavier than a human adult male.

How did the dinosaurs die?

There are several theories as to how the dinosaurs died. These are discussed in chapter 6. Two theories, however, seem to lead the pack. The first is that dinosaurs fell victim to changing climate. The second is that the impact of an asteroid caused devastating, rapid changes on Earth, changes that the dinosaurs could not survive. Many paleontologists believe that the extinction of the dinosaurs was a result of a combination of factors.

Which was the last dinosaur?

The fossil record seems to show a drop in the number of species of dinosaur toward the end of the Cretaceous Period. Dinosaurs were, however, widespread, and the populations of those species that existed at the time were probably large. Ceratopsians and duckbilled dinosaurs were very common during the late Cretaceous. Although it's impossible to say which was the last of the dinosaurs, these groups are likely to have been among them.

Are there any dinosaurs left?

There are stories and legends of Mesozoic creatures that still roam the Earth. The Loch Ness Monster is said to be a primitive, sea-going reptile. Tales of a great beast fitting the description of an *Apatosaurus* are heard in the jungles along the Congo River. As fascinating as they are, these stories are not based on any solid evidence. The last of the dinosaurs is most assuredly long gone.

Did cavemen hunt dinosaurs?

NO!! If humans had existed during the Mesozoic, there is a good chance that in some cases they might have actually been the hunted. Humans and dinosaurs, however, did not coexist. They missed each other by at least 60 million years.

Were there any nice dinosaurs?

By modern standards, there were probably many dinosaurs that could have been considered gentle or appealing, but we can only guess. The behavior of certain types of hadrosaurs may have been much like that of modern deer. Sauropods could have been similar in nature to modern elephants. There is fossil evidence, however, that some species—the *Maiasaura,* for example—were caring parents that fed and protected their young.

These questions form my top 20 list, but your youngster will certainly come up with queries that are not included here. If you don't know an answer, don't hesitate to admit it and then search for it together. The goal is to encourage your son or daughter to ask and then to explore. Through this process, children gain confidence in their ability to find the answers.

A fascination with dinosaurs is a universal magnet that can be used to draw your youngster into the fold of science and scientific thought. By sharing this learning experience, you become a most important key in unlocking your child's imagination and perhaps launching a journey that will last a lifetime. Whether you are searching among the rocks for fossils, scouring a shoreline for pretty shells, or scanning the skies for shooting stars, you will fan the spark of your child's curiosity. Perhaps this point was best stated by nineteenth century essayist and historian Thomas Carlyle:

> *The lightning-spark of Thought, generated or say rather heaven-kindled, in the solitary mind, awakens its likeness in another mind, in a thousand other minds, and all blaze up together in combined fire.*

1

Parks and Museums

The following is a list of notable national parks and museums in the United States and Canada that focus on the dinosaur age and provide a variety of exciting learning opportunities for you and your family. Hours and admission charges vary; call or write for more information.

Arizona

Museum of Northern Arizona
Route 4, P.O. Box 720
Flagstaff, AZ 86001
(602) 774-5211

Petrified Forest National Park
(between Interstate 40 and U.S.
Highway 180)
P.O. Box 2217
Petrified Forest NP, AZ 86028
(602) 524-6228

California

California Academy of Sciences
Golden Gate Park
San Francisco, CA 94118
(415) 221-5100

*Natural History Museum
of Los Angeles County*
900 Exposition Blvd.
Los Angeles, CA 90007
(213) 744-3466

*George C. Page Museum
(at the La Brea Tar Pits)*
5801 Wilshire Blvd.
Los Angeles, CA 90036
(213) 936-2230

*University of California Museum
of Paleontology*
Room 3, Earth Sciences Bldg.,
University of California
Berkeley, CA 94720
(510) 642-1821

Colorado

Denver Museum of Natural History
2001 Colorado Blvd.
Denver, CO 80205
(303) 370-6357

Dinosaur Valley Museum
352 Main St.
Grand Junction, CO 81501
(303) 243-3466

Connecticut

Dinosaur State Park
400 West St.
Rocky Hill, CT 06067
(203) 529-8423

District of Columbia

National Museum of
Natural History
Smithsonian Institution
10th and Constitution Ave. NW
Washington, DC 20560
(202) 357-1300

Peabody Museum
of Natural History
Yale University
170 Whitney Ave.
New Haven, CT 06520
(203) 432-5050

Illinois

Field Museum of Natural History
Lake Shore Dr. and Roosevelt Rd.
Chicago, IL 60605
(312) 922-9410

Kansas

J. Dyche Museum of Natural
History
University of Kansas
Lawrence, KS 66045
(913) 864-4540

Massachusetts

Museum of Comparative Zoology
Harvard University
11 Divinity Ave.
Cambridge, MA 02138
(617) 495-1910

Michigan

University of Michigan
Alexander Ruthven Museums
1109 Geddes Ave.
Ann Arbor, MI 48109
(313) 764-0478

Montana

Museum of the Rockies
Montana State University
Bozeman, MT 59715
(406) 994-5257

Nebraska

Agate Fossil Beds National
Monument
(off Nebraska Route 29)
P.O. Box 27
Gering, NE 69341-0427
(308) 436-4340

New Mexico

Ghost Ranch Conference Center
Ruth Hall Paleontology Room
Albiquiu, NM 87510
(505) 685-4333

New Mexico Museum
of Natural History
1801 Mountain Rd., N.W.
Albuquerque, NM 87104
(505) 841-8836

New York

American Museum of
Natural History
Central Park West at 79th St.
New York, NY 10024-5192
(212) 769-5100

Ohio

Cleveland Museum
of Natural History
1 Wade Oval Dr., University Circle
Cleveland, OH 44106
(216) 231-4600

Oregon

John Day Fossil Beds
National Monument
(2 miles from U.S. Highway 26
on Route 19)
420 East Main
John Day, OR 97845
(503) 987-2333 (park
headquarters)

Pennsylvania

Academy of Natural Sciences
Logan Square, 19th and The
Benjamin Franklin Parkway
Philadelphia, PA 19103
(215) 299-1000

Carnegie Museum
of Natural History
4400 Forbes Ave.
Pittsburgh, PA 15213
(412) 622-3131

South Dakota

Badlands National Park
(off Interstate 90 on
Highway 240)
P.O. Box 6
Interior, SD 57750
(605) 433-5361

Texas

Dinosaur Valley State Park
P.O. Box 396
Glen Rose, TX 76043
(817) 897-4588

Fort Worth Museum of Science
and History
1501 Montgomery St.
Fort Worth, TX 76107
(817) 732-1631

Utah

Dinosaur National Monument
P.O. Box 128
Jensen, UT 84035
(801) 789-2115 (Quarry)

CEU Prehistoric Museum
College of Eastern Utah
451 East 400 North
Price, UT 84501
(801) 637-5060

Earth Sciences Museum
Brigham Young University
Provo, UT 84602
(801) 378-3680

Utah Field House of Natural History
State Park and Dinosaur Gardens
235 E. Main St.
Vernal, UT 84078
(801) 789-3799

Utah Museum of Natural History
University of Utah
Salt Lake City, UT 84112
(801) 581-4303

Wyoming

Fossil Butte National Monument
P.O. Box 592
Kemmerer, WY 83101-0527
(307) 877-4455

Geological Museum
University of Wyoming
P.O. Box 3254
Laramie, WY 82071
(307) 766-4218

CANADA

Alberta

Calgary Zoo and Botanical Society
at Prehistoric Park
P.O. Box 3036, Station B
Calgary, Alberta T2M 4R8
(403) 232-9300

Drumheller Dinosaur and
Fossil Museum
335 1st Street East
Drumheller, Alberta T0J 0Y0
(403) 823-2593

Museum of Paleontology
Field Station
Dinosaur Provincial Park
P.O. Box 60
Patricia, Alberta T0J 2K0
(403) 378-4342

Provincial Museum of Alberta
12845 102 Avenue
Edmonton, Alberta T5N 0M6
(403) 453-9100

Tyrrell Musuem of Paleontology
P.O. Box 7500
Drumheller, Alberta T0J 0Y0
(403) 823-7707

Ontario

Canadian Museum of Nature
P.O. Box 3443, Station D
Ottawa, Ontario K1P 6P4
(613) 996-3102

Royal Ontario Museum
100 Queen's Park
Toronto, Ontario M5S 2C6
(416) 586-5551

Many universities and museums offer fossil-hunting programs for kids and their families to enjoy together. Here are a few of those special opportunities:

- Each year, the Lawrence Hall of Science at the University of California at Berkeley offers a Dino Trek that includes visits to western quarries and museums.

- The Oregon Museum of Science and Industry has a program for kids 13 to 18 years of age. They visit the Hancock Field Station Mammal Quarry where they may participate in a supervised dig.

- The Museum of the Rockies in Montana offers a paleontology field school with a range of opportunities, including two-day introductory sessions and week-long sessions. The base camp, Camp Makela, is located on short-grass prairie 90 miles from Glacier National Park and is made up of 24 Blackfeet Indian tipis that serve as sleeping quarters, a dining hall, warehouses, and classrooms. The two-day session includes field work, lectures, slide shows, and discussions with paleontologists. Kids must be at least 10 years of age and must be accompanied by an adult. Meals are provided. To attend the extended one-week sessions children must be 12 years of age or older.

You can find out more by calling (406) 994-5257 or writing to Dave Swingle, Museum of the Rockies, Montana State University, Bozeman, MT 59715.

2

Further Reading

For Parents

Colbert, Edwin H. *Men and Dinosaurs: The Search in Field and Laboratory.* New York: Dutton, 1968.

Cvancara, Alan M. *Sleuthing Fossils.* New York: Wiley, 1990.

Czerkas, Sylvia J., and Olsen, Everett, C., eds. *Dinosaurs Past and Present.* Los Angeles: Natural History Museum of Los Angeles in association with University of Washington Press, 1987.

Dixon, Dougal; Cox, Barry; Savage, R. J. G.; and Gardiner, Brian. *The Macmillan Illustrated Encyclopedia of Dinosaurs and Prehistoric Animals.* New York: Macmillan, 1988.

Horner, John R. *Digging Dinosaurs.* New York: Harper & Row, 1988.

Lambert, David. *A Field Guide to Dinosaurs.* New York: Avon, 1983.

Lambert, David. *The Field Guide to Prehistoric Life.* New York: Facts On File, 1985.

Norman, David. *The Illustrated Encyclopedia of Dinosaurs.* New York: Crescent Books, 1985.

Sattler, Helen Roney. *The New Illustrated Dinosaur Dictionary.* New York: Lothrop, Lee & Shepard Books, 1983.

Steel, Rodney, and Harvey, Anthony. *The Encyclopedia of Prehistoric Life.* New York: McGraw-Hill, 1979.

For Children

Adler, David A. *The Dinosaur Princess and Other Prehistoric Riddles.* New York: Bantam, 1990.

Aliki. *Digging Up Dinosaurs.* New York: Thomas Y. Crowell, 1981.

Aliki. *Dinosaur Bones.* New York: Thomas Y. Crowell, 1988.

Arnold, Caroline. *Dinosaur Mountain—Graveyard of the Past.* New York: Clarion Books, 1988.

Berger, Melvin. *Stranger Than Fiction—Dinosaurs.* New York: Avon, 1990.

Booth, Jerry. *The Big Beast Book.* Boston: Little, Brown, 1988.

Branley, Frank M. *Dinosaurs, Asteroids & Superstars.* New York: Thomas Y. Crowell, 1982.

Carrick, Carol. *Patrick's Dinosaurs.* New York: Clarion Books, 1983.

Daeschler, Ted. *Start Collecting Fossils.* Philadelphia: Running Press, 1988.

Elting, Mary, and Goodman, Ann. *Dinosaur Mysteries.* New York: Grosset & Dunlap, 1980.

Freedman, Russell. *Dinosaurs and Their Young.* New York: Holiday House, 1983.

Gregory, Niles, and Eldredge, Douglas. *The Fossil Factory.* New York: Addison-Wesley, 1989.

Horner, John, and Gorman, James. *Maia: A Dinosaur Grows Up.* Philadelphia: Running Press, 1989.

McMullan, Kate. *Dinosaur Hunters.* New York: Random House, 1989.

Peters, David. *A Gallery of Dinosaurs & Other Early Reptiles.* New York: Alfred A. Knopf, 1989.

Sattler, Helen Roney. *Baby Dinosaurs.* New York: Lothrop, Lee & Shepard Books, 1984.

Wexo, John. *Prehistoric Zoobooks.* San Diego: Wildlife Education, Ltd., 1989.

Field Guides

Dietrich, R. V., and Wicander, Reed. *Minerals, Rocks, and Fossils: A Self-Teaching Guide.* New York: Wiley, 1983.

Horenstein, Sidney, ed. *Simon and Schuster's Guide to Fossils.* New York: Simon and Schuster, 1986.

Horenstein, Sidney. *The Audubon Society Pocket Guide: Familiar Fossils; North America.* New York: Alfred A. Knopf, 1988.

McDonald, J. R. *Fossils for Amateurs: Paleontology Field Guide.* New York: Van Nostrand Reinhold, 1983.

Moody, Richard. *Fossils.* New York: Macmillan, 1986.

Murray, Marian. *Hunting for Fossils: A Guide to Finding and Collecting Fossils in All Fifty States.* New York: Macmillan, 1967 (paperback 1974).

Pellant, Chris. *Rocks, Minerals & Fossils of the World.* Boston: Little, Brown, 1990.

Ransom, J. E. *Fossils in America.* New York: Harper & Row, 1964.

Rhoads, F. H. T.; Zim, H. S.; and Schaffer, P. R. *Fossils: A Guide to Prehistoric Life.* New York: Golden Press, 1962.

Thompson, Ida. *Audubon Society Field Guide to North American Fossils.* New York: Alfred A. Knopf, 1982.

Index